Butt Naked

Raw

&

Uncensored!

The Book of Truth

Thanks for the Support!

Sadiki Ross
(Steven Danzy, Jr.)

Butt Naked

Raw

&

Uncensored!

The Book of Truth

Essays, Articles, Retrospective and Poetry

By Sadiki Bakari

Introduction by Moya Mzuri Pambeli

Published by Sadiki Bakari
First Printing 2007
ISBN: 978-0-6151-5261-5
Printed in the **United Snakes of AmeriKKKa**

www.sadikibakari.com

Edited by Shay Ensley
Co-edited by Sadiki Bakari

Cover Design and Photo by:
Black Star Photography

Dedication

This book is dedicated to my Mother and Father, to Elijah and Negussay as well as my immediate family, extended family and comrades in the struggle: The Nappy Tongue Vanguard, The F.T.P Movement, Guerrilla Republik, All Afrikans People's Revolutionary Party, P.O.C.C, Black Riders, The Moors, U.N.I.A and those unnamed. This does not mean that they endorse all, or part of the information in this book. On this journey of truth I summon and pay homage to the ancestors who fought, lived and went on to the ancestral realm for our freedom and liberation with all of their being to speak through me. I'm a server of the people so I also dedicate the spirit of this book to the dehumanized, downtrodden and oppressed victimized by this Gestapo government and fascist system of global white supremacy. This book is also dedicated to the Afrikans who suffered the worst atrocity and so-called holocaust in all of history, the European Slave Trade and persecution! May my spirit and the reading of this book become part of your subconscious. Last but not least, Shay Fresh. You are the epitome and manifestation of Goddess state.

CONTENTS

Retrospective

The Word

Epilogue 151

WARNING!
This book may liberate you!

Possible Side Effects:
Truth
A profound love for your people
A deeper sense of self
Increase in social awareness
Political Incorrectness
Hatred of the System
Graduate from Religion
Clarity
Transformation
Revolution

Preface

This book will piss you off and fearlessly evoke the warrior in you. The purpose is to enlighten you and not to offend you, but to expose and confront one's deepest fears. These thoughts are so cutting edge and controversial, I had difficulties finding someone to write a foreword, even with some of the so-called or considered controversial black intellectuals that exist. The embodiment of this work will vividly and descriptively show you the mange and filth of this 'sweet land of liberty'. These essays, articles, retrospectives and poems aren't docile, timid or passive. This book was written for the masses of oppressed people but more specifically written for Afrikans in the Diasporas. *Butt Naked, Raw & Uncensored* will probably be one of the most controversial books in the years to come simply because these writings are beyond fearless and dares to address topics considered politically incorrect and taboo in Amerikkkan society and history. It will broaden the scope of one's thought process and compel us to struggle for clarity. The truth has absolutely no color lines or racial barriers; the only barriers being the constraints of one's mind. This book courageously discusses the blatant western hegemony, homosexuality in the form of sexual terrorism, religious belief systems falsely interpreted as spirituality, as well as the meticulous love I feel for the Afrikan woman. It is always important for her angelic being, intellect, gentleness, beauty and her warrior spirit to be magnified and immortalized properly.

Keep in mind this quote by Neely Fuller as you read this book, "If you do not understand White Supremacy (Racism)-what it is, and how it works-everything else that you understand, will only confuse you." This is a necessity in overstanding black love, Amerikkka the psychopath, forced assimilation, social rearing, the role of the artist and Global White Supremacy in general. I'm very precise in terminology. If it is a crackkka, I call it a crakkka. If it is racism, I call it racism. If they are psychopaths, I call them psychopaths and if they are slaves, I call them slaves. This book exists outside the lines of any westernized construct whether it is belief system, paradigm or theory. The European slave trade was not our beginning and most definitely will not be our end.

Butt Naked, Raw & Uncensored will force you to think critically and analytically and to take a serious look at yourself, Amerikkka the ugly and beautiful, genocide, fascism and the outright dirty bastards in government. The real gangsters wear suits and ties and lie to you publicly in the media and are connected to the greatest atrocities, war crimes, economic scandals and crimes against humanity the world has ever witnessed and this is why the brutally honest truth must be conveyed and *uncensored*. We must manifest the truth and it shall be. Reader, you will encounter the dialectical laws of opposites in a wide range of topics. This is a process and I affirm with every fiber of my being that these writings will assist us in that process. The vision of this book is to dismantle inferiority complexes and self-hate, to create and elevate social consciousness and awareness in the aspects of black love, spirituality, politics, history and culture and to finally create a medium that tells the truth to our youth. Simply put...this book bitch-slaps the power structure!

Introduction
by Moya Mzuri Pambeli

This backwards-settler, colonial-capitalist government has known, felt and tasted the strength and power of some of the most dynamic and revolutionary youth ever to have attacked any system and they had to face those young revolutionaries from the moment they confronted us in Africa and then in Haiti, Jamaica and throughout the Diaspora. But here in amerika in the 1950's-70's the struggle and strugglers created youth and organization that together challenged this illegal government and threatened to bring it to its knees. We (our African community here in amerika) produced strong unyielding revolutionary youth of the Civil Rights and Human Rights movement, Negroes with and without guns from New Dixie to New York, from the Black Power movement to Black Panthers from New Africans to the Pan African movement and all those in between.

Since then, the media has spent the last few decades trying to destroy that seed (with drugs, imprisonment, joblessness), tried to destroy that revolutionary consciousness and undermine the social/cultural, political and economic development of our African communities both at home in Africa and abroad. They have tried to feed us crack, consumerism and all the trappings of capitalism to create ideological, spiritual and material mutations of African dysfunctionalism and some of this has worked to our detriment. They have been working on all forms of social reconstruction and social destruction using media for re/mis-education to create the regressive social, ideological and cultural reactionary or counter revolutionary milieu for this *next generation,* but by understanding the laws of nature, they have also created the dialectical opposite.

One can not change what has happened to a people. Our past (both good and bad) has created the genetic DNA component of resistance, struggle and revolution and it is regenerated every generation. Thus, our generations will continue this struggle and this journey. Our response will be on every level, social-ideological, political, economic and cultural. For every action there is an equal and/or greater reaction…and that is a fact. We are who we are and so this life-struggle, resistance, victories and defeats of Cultural Revolution and Political Revolution has continued and will continue to give birth to the Next Generation of revolutionary voices of struggle, resistance, and rebuilding.

Introducing Sadiki Bakari.

Sadiki is among the thousands (perhaps millions) of young voices who represent an aspect of this generation's struggle to right the wrongs, to develop new revolutionary consciousness and seek the Truth. Seeking the truth not just for individual enlightenment or self-aggrandizement (ego), which are pervasive in this society and especially amongst so-called conscious males in the movement. But his voice, his work, his contribution (from what I have witnessed in our community) is to build on revolutionary consciousness from our past, present and contribute to a victorious future...building on Ourstory rather than his-story. The consciousness of new revolutionary awakening on the level of spiritual, cultural, historical, social, political and economic development and expansion as a people. That which will bring forth the New Revolutionary Mass World Order to come must confront, address and destroy the old corrupt globalizing world order that in its own contradictory nature will contribute to its own destruction while being dismantled through the People's struggle.

Sadiki's body of work covers all stations, flips all channels and if you don't stay tuned, you might just miss the intent of it all. It leaves very few stones unturned and avoids political correctness. We talk about it (those unmentionable subjects) amongst ourselves, but we try to avoid these subjects in public because it makes us (or our neighbor) uncomfortable and thus the liberalism grows and our development socially is held back. However, the issues do not disappear and the symptoms/conditions actually get worse. That is why this work is so important. It is his analysis, some history and strongly African-centered, but perhaps a more Afro-centric analysis that is bringing some balance to a heavily Eurocentric world that dominates every medium in our lives. This is a beginning and not the end; the first book or the final answer to the questions many of the youth and some of us elders are struggling over. The ideas mentioned need to be on the table and rightly so. He has done that and it is an important step and an important contribution.

Revolution is not reform. Revolution is rapid, thorough, complete, systematic and unapologetic total change. Kwame Nkrumah tells us that revolution is not changing a few things here and there. It is the complete destruction of the corrupt system of exploiting one human over another for profit and rebuilding a new society based on equality and respect for people's culture, people's creativity and people's well being with that of nature. Revolutionary Balance.

There will be no order or balance until everything is taken apart and then put back together-in our interest, in the interest of humanity and especially for African People in the order in which our new revolutionary culture/needs dictate. We will need to build a new understanding of religion, social and cultural resurrection of all indigenous people's culture, sex, politics, family structure and relations (and male/female relationships), identity, government, education and more. All this, including institutions and relationships will have to be re-examined, redefined, and re-developed in the interest of the masses of our people for the building of our new society. This is why Sadiki's body of work presented to us is so unapologetically refreshing and so very relevant today. This is what has stopped me in my tracks…to not miss one line, one word or one statement in hopes of not misinterpreting what is being said and I suggest to the reader that you do the same. What he offers is serious, enlightening and challenges much of what we understand to be our history or our place in the world today. It's an important statement. I believe that no matter what your opinion or understanding is, take your time with this work. The issues are important and the emotions are sincere. The intent I believe is to encourage discussion and debate and to pull the rug back. Let's get busy….It's Nation building!

It is naked, raw and un-censored so that we can feel the magnitude of his/our anger, his/our love, his/our soft-core and hard-core, revealing his political manifesto! We feel the seriousness and intensity of it all. The beauty of his love and respect for the African woman, acknowledging every part of our being and our strength and exalting us to our rightful place where we have reigned in her-story and will continue reign as the first Wo-man; revealing our place as the first people, the greatest contributors to world civilization, yet so many of us do not know our own story. Let's tell it like it is!

Like China (in the era of Mao Tse-Tung), our community and our youth need to launch a cultural revolution where (among other issues) we give and show true Ra-spect for the Elder, the young and especially the African Wo-man instead of mimicking this backwards society.

Sadiki's language is raw. Yes, he is calling a spade a spade and a capitalist cracker a capitalist cracker! Do you know who your enemy is? Many of us don't. He is standing up for our African and other revolutionary struggles from Haiti to Palestine to West Papua to the land of the Dine! Condemning them and challenging US to destroy capitalism, imperialism, neo-colonialism, Zionism, the enemies of all justice-loving people and to also destroy those backward ideological and cultural tendencies that we have acquired. I reflect on the spiritual revelations, both the cultural and political that our-story offered, without cosmetic under or overtones, addressing our grave problems without the political correctness or liberal apologies. Straight up-no chaser truth - that is what we need and what we get in his/our Butt Naked truth! Whether we agree or not, we must be open to discuss, debate and/or struggle to come to some common understanding because that is how we as a people and as individuals will continue to grow. Growing pains like birth pains can be uncomfortable, but we shouldn't be afraid of a little pain considering the great suffering we have gone through for centuries to get where we are. From the aspect of our struggle and our existence, the political, social and cultural prison that we have been locked down behind for hundreds of years both mental and physical will require years of reassessment and rebuilding. For this generation and the next, this work contributes to that process.

Sadiki expresses the evolutionary and revolutionary transformation of consciousness of the new generation of Revolutionaries and the direction they must venture towards. Totally militant, but also not afraid to get deeply reflective and spiritual, openly reclaiming our identity, spiritual and cultural past and our national and international position in World Civil–I-zation! Sekou Toure reminds us that "As Man seeks the happiness of his society and continually climbs towards perfection necessarily leading to the infinite consolidation of his internal and external equilibrium, seeking development and harmony, it should characterize the *moral objective of the conditions of one's life* and move towards the continual improvement of his relationships with the society in which he lives and acts."(*Africa on the Move*, page 20). This is to say that when we live and develop among the people as social beings struggling for truth, seeking balance and justice, we must examine every aspect of our lives both *personal and political* and the lives of our people. Many so-called revolutionaries in the movement have terrible personal relationships and believe that the political revolution is only in external relationships and their personal behavior can be totally reactionary. What is manifested within reflects in all relationships both internal and external. Sadiki understands that and on his journey he is offering these reflections for all of us to look at and address.

Is our cultural base from Africa or Europe? Should the foundation of our moral and ethical understanding come from Russia, Rome or Kemet? This is new territory for the new African Revolutionary. Check our moral balance in personal relationships, egos, social relationships, integrity, image of self in total balance, chauvinism, our spirituality or lack of it. Note that revolutionaries usually ignore this aspect of struggle (the relationship of consciousness/spirit) seeking pure Marxist analysis of pure materialism. But dialectically speaking, if all life is both material and immaterial then we must master both aspects of our-selves which include the consciousness, thoughts and ideas that guide us (or spirit).

Sadiki is a brave young voice bringing forth a new voice of consciousness in a creative New African form to address many old issues, problems, struggles and yet he IS young and has a young spirit and is reaching the next generation. This work, his contribution is a beginning in the right direction. It is by any means necessary, a work for change. Change for a new generation by fighting for liberation. Change to reject the old, corrupt colonial mentality and structure. The daring and bravery of the young is a reminder that we too were young and challenged the world and our own community with this same tenacity. We have one revolutionary culture and consciousness which is ever expanding and impacting our struggle and armed with this revolutionary culture. We have WON many battles and WILL win the war if we demand it, speak it into being and LIVE IT. We are at War and every medium we have at our disposal MUST BE used in the battle for our awakening consciousness towards the organizing of a new society. Sadiki is making his contribution and we say Medase, asante sana - to the ancestors, the parents, elders, youth and all who have helped in his development and his journey. This is just the beginning and he will have more to say and more to contribute for his people. We look forward to his voice, his life, and our journey to liberation.

One God, One Aim, One Destiny!
Africa and Africans must be free, United and Socialist!

Forward ever! Backwards Never!

Moya Mzuri Pambeli
All African People's Revolutionary Party
All African Women's Revolutionary Union

"Under the system of racism/white supremacy,
it is incorrect to say that any person
except a racist/white supremacist has died of natural causes!"

ALLEN STIMPSON

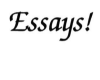

Essays!

Guilty

We clearly and accurately visualize that homeland security has manifested into homeland insecurity as we see this government's tobacco spitting cowboys, its lackeys and cronies paranoia to uphold rightwing conservative totalitarian Gestapo ideology and practice. No one is as *THUG* and *GANGSTER* as the red, white and blue star spangled banner pledge of allegiance to hierarchy golf playing mob bosses, the KKK in suits instead of white sheets on tactical alert. Patriot's Acts, Anti-Terrorism Bills and manufactured laws are being mandated under the illusion of foreign threats to the people's so-called freedom. The monumental threat we see is police terrorism, especially since the rogue pigs protect government property and jurisdiction and not the service of the people. Martial law and police state has been quietly implemented. Human and civil liberties have been a gross contradiction and negligence. The similarities between Nazi Germany and this government are so profound they could be an analogy for identical twins.

The dichotomy of republicans and democrats are the same party with different methods yet the same results. It's time to dismantle the hidden hand and bent wrist of global white supremacy aided by this new pimp reform of neo-capitalism, imperialism and fascism, all beasts of the amerikkkan patriarchs and their dubious economic and political elitism in this so-called Christian nation. Ain't nobody singing, "My country tis of thee, sweet land of liberty." Past slave masters and colonialists willed their offspring the oppressive state, diseased money and slave blood. This global psychopathic sickness of white supremacy boosts their inferiority complex hidden under Uncle Sam's lice hat.

These are the same villains that infiltrated our melanin and neighborhoods with crack, ousted President Aristide out of Haiti and if not for Maxine Waters he probably would've been assassinated under mysterious circumstances. 1st Amendment rights have been colonized and now the 1st Amendment speaks like a house niggaz tongue with an agenda and no apology. There is a documented contingent that the UNITED SNAKES GOVERNMENT are

Uncensored!

the TERRORISTS and globally the war on terror is against communalism, socialism, pan afrikanism, egalitarianism and a people's government or system of being. Afrikans in Amerikkka have always been terrorized and it isn't by Muslims, Al Qaeda or the Taliban as they claim. It is by the ancestors of these white folk here in this country and their descendants implement the same kind of terror today.

This government is guilty of war crimes, air strikes in Pakistan, wire tapping scandals, mass genocide, dictatorship, bogus propaganda, false imprisonments, misappropriation of wealth, religious imperialism and conquest, ghetto concentration camps, coup d' états, gentrification, corporate looting, invading Afghanistan, Iraq, Vietnam, Lebanon, too many Afrikan countries to mention in one article, threats to invade Iran, Cuba, Venezuela and Korea, guilty of stealing elections, diamond mines, oil, resources in general, guilty of sweatshops, food, water and medical deprivation, illegal occupations, capitalism, unemployment, national debts, colonialism, cultism and historical terrorism. So, you tell me who is guilty of cleverly propagating the IMF "international monetary fund" and the WTO "world trade organization" or how about the World Bank? These are only a few examples of terrorists who happen to slander its opposition's resistance as terrorism.

We must oppose and expose the United Snakes Government by pulling down its pants not only for its satanic tendencies but their dehumanizing global oppressive contraband. We must no longer be puppets in this bourgeois class system that keeps its foot and cave club on our plight since everything is politics when dictated by this opportunistic ruling ass and class. Our 40 acres and a mule became 40-Ounces, vagrancy laws and the industrial prison complex. The crooked bourgeois government hinders global consciousness and distorts the people's reality. The system keeps strait-jackets on the workers' self-determination. This fallacious international fascism straightens our nappy hair systemically as they still worship, raise and wave their confederate demonic gay flags in the oval office. We often are desensitized to this government's Nazi ties, the Bush family and Hitler, Kerry, Arnold Schwarzenegger as well as its secret society makeup and demonic ritualistic traditions, new world order speeches, Zionist protocol, hidden and distorted symbolism,

Uncensored!

fraud constitution and mind control that misguides revolutionary consciousness and revolutionary socialism. We must exploit their erroneous dogmas and bare witness to true freedom and God state. Didn't the Indians tell us the white man speaks with a fork tongue, so don't u think he thinks, writes and govern with one as well? Free the people, Free Afrika, Free all political prisoners and bang on na' system. May yo' tongue stay nappy!!!!!!!!

Sexual Terrorism

This is a taboo subject that the majority of writers, so-called scholars, artists and clergymen refuse to deal with due to their cowardice; AmeriKKKa's social rearing and forced tolerance perpetrated by the media as well as the hidden aspects of this government that embrace homosexuality. But, this book is called 'Butt Naked, Raw and Uncensored' for a reason. Political correctness is a cancer in this society and society needs a full body cleanse, if there were more of an abundance of political incorrectness there would be prophetic dialogue, reasoning, conclusive results and most importantly, truth. This historical perversion has been the demise of many civilizations usually after European colonization and will be one of the downfalls of this land that I dare not call civilization. As John Henrik Clarke stated, "In order to have civilization one must first be civil." The rise in homosexuality is the decline and soon destruction of civilization. We know that the mating of animals is less bestial, inhumane and vile than homosexuality. They have more of an overstanding of balance, instinct, intuition and the sense of depopulating than some men and women. All we have to do is look at the history of European sexual behavior. The behavior in Greece and Rome wasn't any different than their behavior in the caves of the Caucasus Mountains. Greeks had a profound hatred towards women. They saw women as dirty, disgusting and wretched. They felt in Greek culture that a woman's menstrual cycle was demonic and satanic. Many of them preferred have sex with little boys for their initiation or with animals like sheep if one even considers this sex. They've always had festivals and celebrations to support this, Easter being one of them. Their own historians and so-called philosophers document this. This wasn't Afrikan culture and at this present time this culture has been imposed by the oppressor on their slaves. I don't really need to go into further detail about the sexual deviancy of Greece and Rome. Research it for yourself. It's very clear and an indisputable fact that their descendants are the elite and controllers of white supremacy which rears social behavior and creates a

Uncensored!

tolerance for their neurotic gender desecration and gender exploitation. Mass manipulation and propaganda is crucial in the desensitizing of the people. They make it seem to be an issue of tolerance and rights as oppose to the issue of perversion, morals or even terrorism.

We are often bombarded by the term "terrorism". Let's take it to another level. Homosexuality is *SEXUAL TERRORISM!* Why won't this government have the media call it that? The government uses this distorted behavior as a means of contraceptive or birth control for depopulation and genocide especially for blacks or people with melanin. This is another way of stopping the black messiah from rising and taking his and her rightful thrown and place in society. The feminization of the black male tears apart the balance and essence of the black family structure not to mention the emotional and spiritual castration of the black female. This only confuses our children to have parents of the same sex and this is far worse than any other scenario. We need more Afrikan centered black psychologists to stand up against this perversion and terrorism. This European culture contradicts their heralded naturalists. Homosexuals or "species of organism" would be considered inferior species according to Darwinism, due to their incapability to reproduce and without reproduction homosexuals could not survive. They themselves prove that homosexuality is against nature and Darwin's theory of evolution. Of course I'm not by any means a Darwinist but AmeriKKKa seems to love Darwin so I thought I'd use him as an example. How can we actualize illumination when practicing deviant behavior and culture? Why is this not a moral issue yet this country has the audacity to invade foreign places under the auspice of their immorality? This type of moral genocide gnaws at the soul of sacred innocence and purity. Sodomy, molestation, pedophilia and rape are also aspects of SEXUAL TERRORISM. This sexual retardation disrupts procreation and the concept of Goddess and God but I guess you would have to be one to innerstand this.

Maybe if we fought for human rights instead of civil rights we wouldn't have assisted gays in receiving rights for their role in the destruction of humanity, gender and morality. We didn't recognize that the government didn't have a problem with their own demonic culture being further elevated by an unaware society just as eventually they allowed blacks to integrate and yes, they allowed it. It wasn't forced. The same form of government still exists, right? What happened to our black owned businesses after that? We want to be so socially accepted by AmeriKKKan culture that some of us willingly give up our spirit, soul, masculinity, femininity, Afrikan family structure and values and make pacts with these terrorists and carry out their sexual rituals. We allow negative socialization and condemnation when we speak against it. Many of you would think it's conspiracy theory if I said this government kidnaps 4 year olds and force them to be homosexual sex slaves in and outside of the government to put certain people in compromising positions in order to blackmail (whitemail) them. What type of society and culture would force people to be sex slaves especially children? Don't think for one second that religions aren't involved in this warfare and deviancy. Gender role reversal is covert warfare especially those the war has been declared on. Some of these clerics validate *SEXUAL TERRORISM* in their writings and teachings even though we haven't heard of any messiahs or prophets having parents of the same sex but we know all "religion" is contradictory anyway. Read my article on Spirituality vs. Religion. We've allowed these neurotic and insane behaviors to infiltrate our chakra energy. I hope one doesn't think this elevates our connection with the universe. This *SEXUAL TERRORISM* is a blatant attack on the Afrikan concept of balance which is rooted in the principles of Maat which are spiritual principles. Yes, homosexuality declares war on the spirit; especially the spirit of the original man and woman of all humanity. This is a direct attack on cosmic law and its feminine and masculine principles. This is a soulless behavior deified by these uncivilized people and many of us have become products and slaves to this savage lifestyle. What's next? Their false white depiction of Jesus already looks gay. Will their false depiction of the white Mary or Madonna soon look masculine or better yet will the trinity be two white men and child or two white women and child because in this society wouldn't it be politically incorrect to challenge this? For those of you who will say this is hate due to your cowardice and brainwashing, this isn't hate. This is love for natural order and the laws of the universe and nature which many people are in

10

compliance with as oppose to man's belief and law which others are in compliance with. Some of you are fucking slaves! In deviant states we lose all concepts of God and Goddess and allow all different forms of terrorism to slowly kill us including *SEXUAL TERRORISM.* You have been forewarned!

*"Morality dwells in the core of our spirit
But immorality often tries to visit!"*

Sadiki Bakari

Spirituality vs. Re-ligion

Why are many of us afraid to be hue-man? It's your birth right. To be hue-man is to be free. Religion is imperialism, capitalism, colonialism, slavery and oppression and that isn't humanity. All RELIGIONS are Euro "peons" poor reincarnations of true Afrikan spirituality. Spirituality or Spirit is innate and part of our natural make-up. Religion is institutional and material based with social constructs. A social rearing that binds and oppresses the animation of spirit and the actualization of soul transmigration. We are born with spirit and God state when man and woman bring forth the thought of being into existence. Someone imposes or gives one religion after the birth process. Conformity is imposed and so are man-made religions and all of them are included. NO RELIGION is exempt or excluded. Islam is no better than Christianity and its gang bangin' cross. These man made written books the source of true spiritual independence. Religion creates dependency and in no way should be seen as or characterized as spirituality. The Quran, Bible, Talmud, Veda and whatever other religious books misinterpreted and manipulated by these religious zealots are only a nursery school center to spirituality if a center at all. This is why many of these pimps…I mean Negro slave preachers, clerics, pastors, popes, ministers and priests won't deal with true revolution. They're too busy passing the basket around 4 or 5 times and trying to be politically correct while working with the enemy and inviting the enemy to forums about our freedom and solutions to our problems caused by this capitalistic system and the religious war mongers that perpetuate it under the guise of freedom and eternal life. In order to free ourselves of imperialism, colonialism and capitalism, one must be free of religion which was founded on these hallmarks.

They take money from the enemy and compromise with the enemy. They must be identified. Any so-called religious building that isn't based on Afrikan spirituality and the liberation of our minds; body and soul need to be dismantled because religious doctrine further enslaves slaves. How can you put a man or institution above and beyond your own humanity and divinity? A

Uncensored!

white man at that and then go so far to say color doesn't matter. It mattered to your oppressor. They made sure they manifested him as white and parishioners go to church and worship this melanin-calcified molester and sodomizer.

Religion in general has a great hatred and disposition toward the woman. How can Islam be so patriarchal to initially worship the feminine principle called Al-lat to changing it to the masculine called Allah? It's Europeanism at its best and most Muslims aren't aware of this important fact since they're so busy being programmed by false information they deem to be truth which is really belief. They even refer to themselves as believers and others as non-believers. Religion at best promotes sectarianism. That would mean narrow mindedness. Belief and faith will never set us free physically, psychologically or spiritually. It doesn't take a so-called messiah or prophet to figure that out. Look outside at the state of humanity. Religion will only deal with their skewed paradigm and not a critical/analytical one. One with no religious affiliation can be free of social conformity, rearing and norms. Islam plagiarizes European Christianity which plagiarized Ancient Afrikan Spiritual Concepts and co-opted and distorted them. Mohammed is simply to Islam what Jesus is to Christianity. This isn't an attack on religion but this is a spanking to religious bourgeoisie and arrogance. They exploit, pimp and profit off of religion and call it Spirituality.

The imposter Jews farce of history isn't even worth talking about. Michael Bradley and Friedman documents that vehemently. Any elementary researcher knows you must deal with ancient Afrikan history to even begin to overstand and innerstand biblical teachings, allegory and parables. The question is how can one not give credence to the numerous writings written by Afrikans thousands of years before these modern co-opted, distorted, rewritten, reversed, reworked and expunged euro "peon" man-made books that are obviously the words of man and not 'God' as I use the term loosely. These many religious slaves prefer to live their lives according to their oppressors' misinterpretation, misunderstanding, mis-education and manipulation as oppose to the authors of hue-manity, civilization and the first to embrace their spirit as oppose to enslave it.

Simple questions: How many times has the so-called Word of God been changed by man? What would that make Man? How many times have the Bible been changed and if the Creator is all things then wouldn't the creator be the devil too? Was it God who moved the creation story from one location to another location? Would that mean God doesn't know what the fuck he is talking about? I'm only basing this off the premise that God is a man only according to religion. Yeah, right! Was it God that gave Mark, Matthew, Luke and John 4 different resurrection stories (accounts), but if none of them were there, wouldn't that be considered gossip or hearsay? If both Mary's were there, why don't they have an account of the resurrection in the Bible? Is God racist because biblical passages in religious books are? Why are so many books of the Bible in the Quran? Why were so many parts of the Bible and Quran already written? How could men have ecumenical conferences to rewrite and change the so-called words of God? Was God at those conferences? So-called Jews took the place of God at the Conference at Jamnia in 90 A.D. Do we need to mention all of the blatant racism in the Talmud? Did Jehovah or Yahweh write that or man? Did the so-called Jews simply hijack Afrikan history and claim it for themselves? Have you heard of Khazaria? I could write a book on that alone. Who suppressed Goddess concept and why? What happened to the Book of Mary? According to the scripture, wasn't she born of an immaculate conception prior to Jesus? Why wasn't she considered the savior child? Sisters, you ought to be ashamed of yourselves and outright hate yourselves to not see the image of yourselves as divinity. Why does RELIGION separate you from God? Isn't Judaism, Islam and Christianity similar just interpreted differently by those members of it? Was man religious before religion existed? Hasn't spirituality always existed? Can you put a date on it? Why isn't everyone born of the rib of a man? Have you ever seen a man give birth? Did you see Adam give birth? Have you ever seen a woman give birth from her rib? Have you ever seen Jesus? Then how do you know he exists? Where's the body? Have you ever seen a physical body ascend to so-called Heaven? Has anyone ever come from Heaven or Hell and told you about it? When is Jesus coming back? I guess this is when knowledge...I mean blind faith comes into play. What about those that were here long before the so-called 2000 year old Jesus (or however old) being that they keep changing his birth date? Are they damned to the Hell that they say exists? How do you explain the saviors before him like Asar, Heru, Ptah, Krishna, Buddha, Nomo, Quetzalcoatl, etc? If the image of God's only son is white, doesn't that make everyone else the son of white folk or even the devil and what does that make women? Is there any mention of God having a daughter? Was God misogynistic and patriarchal and if you hate the woman you would have to be homosexual right? Why are there so many sects of Christianity and Islam? Do Muslims really know who Mohammed was and what did he and his parents worship? Most importantly, who was Bilal according to the so-called history? Wasn't he an Afrikan slave and who enslaved him? Wasn't the Hadith written after Mohammed's death just like the gospels written after the so-called death of Jesus? Did Mohammed ever exist or was he just a representation of the cosmological sun? Is Mohammed the Islam's Jesus? Why was El for Elohim taken out of their prayers? *The Asiatic Blackman*? Isn't Islam based in faith and belief as oppose to truth? We do recognize that these aren't the same things referring to faith, belief and truth. Don't they consider members believers? In order to read the Quran all one would have to do is read the Bible or better yet learn ancient Afrikan cosmology. Aren't the allegories practically the same with different names and places? Don't be mad at me. Be mad at yourself for not seeking truth and researching and investigating what you deem to be truth. All of this sounds like the imagination of Europeans. That is why these questions point out so many contradictions in religion's foundation of belief and faith. Religion isn't based on KNOWLEDGE. Man's belief and lack of spirituality breathes life into religion and religion is our spiritual and divine death. It's the assassination of hue-manity and morality. Anytime one suppresses, represses and oppresses the light and balance of femininity, one desecrates humanity and the maturation of it. The suppression of the woman, especially the Afrikan woman is an uncivil, immoral and inhumane society, hence AmeriKKKa. Religion manifests that, so to all the religious robots, white people still call you Nigga as you worship their imperialistic white religions and man-made fraud white image male Deities. Do you ever think of balance and God having the attributes of man and woman or better

Uncensored!

yet, in order to have a God there must be a Goddess or do you think it was some gay God that created water, flowers, sensitivity, rainbows, the color pink and things that are obviously feminine oriented like nurturing and nature.

Spirituality existed eons before Europeans conquering disposition. This is man's imposition called Religion. Spirituality is oneness with the universe and the all-in-one energy, not separatism. How many different man-made forms of religion exist? How many sects and branches exist and why can they all be traced back to the Ancient Spiritual Concepts of divine gnosis in the Nile Valley? It's a very poor interpretation of course. How many sects or branches of spirituality are there? You shouldn't have to think about that question. Some of you still won't get it and will stay sleep for the rest of your lives. It's man's ego and need for greed and control that disconnects ones' spirit, soul and Maa Kheru "true of voice" that transcends the physical realm. You will never truly fight to dismantle your oppressor or their system when you see your oppressor as the image of God. How could you fight against what you subconsciously and visually see and interpret God as? You would subconsciously interpret yourself as the devil in doing that and act as such which is to act out the manifestation of your oppressor which is inhumane. In the words of Dr. Frances Cress Welsing, "The most disastrous aspect of colonization which you are the most reluctant to release from your mind is their colonization of the image of God." Was anyone ever born with a religion? The answer is <u>NO</u> and I dare some idiot to dispute that. We were all born with spirit, some more than others (melanin) and the only thing that severs our umbilical cord to the universe is religion. Some of us are slaves in our own minds and at this point our own enemies. In order to be free one important thing we must do is free ourselves of <u>RELIGION</u>. Your mind through your 3rd eye is the gateway to the universe and true humanity. Why allow it to be separated? Remember, we already created language, the arts, sciences, civilization, etc. before any religion existed; and long before your oppressor even had the ability to speak. How many of you religious slaves truly live the life of the savior you profess to worship? If so, you would all be revolutionaries right?! May yo' tongue stay nappy!

Uncensored!

Psychopathic Amerikkkan Culture
'Don Imus'

Before indulging into psychopathic Amerikkkan culture and Don Imus, I wanted to quote Caucasian author Michael Bradley from his book entitled, 'The Iceman Inheritance Prehistoric Sources of Western Man's Racism, Sexism and Aggression.' "I will attempt to show that racism itself is a predisposition of but one race of Mankind – the white race. I believe that I can show that our converging contemporary crisis, like racism itself, have the origins in the prehistory of the white race alone. We attribute various threats to our survival to 'Man's' folly'…but this is a conscious and self-protecting euphemism. Nuclear war, environmental pollution and resource rape… all are primary threats to our survival and all are the result of peculiarly Caucasoid behaviour, Caucasoid values and Caucasoid psychology. There is no way to avoid the truth. The problem with the world is white men." I think you know where I'm going with this!

Don Imus' insults in regards to Afrikan (black) women being nappy headed hoes are no surprise. Hasn't this been the history of Amerikkkan racist rhetoric and action? Why are we surprised that this psychopathic Amerikkkan culture speaks its most suppressed, in the closet, closed-door boardroom feelings about Black women or men in public forums? They have always trained others to do this as well. Obviously, he represents that culture. Let me be very clear. These comments coming from a white man is blatant racism and an inferiority complex; if these comments came from a black man, it is imposed behavior, self-hate and the lack of knowledge of self. It's amazing how we allow the victimizer to blame the victim for their obviously racial epithets. Isn't it interesting that sexism, dehumanization, oppression, racism, misogyny, patriarchy, poverty, rape and lynching existed before so-called Hip-Hop. Their psychological and physical aggression towards others and themselves is well documented but Don Imus blames Hip-Hop culture or a certain aspect of Hip-Hop which is influenced by the immorality of Amerikkkan culture for his dehumanizing statements?

Uncensored!

Isn't this the same thing the slave master did? Didn't they (white amerikkka) determine that blacks were less than human so they could say or do anything they desired? This is the racist culture and climate they created. Remember, they used the smaller brain scenario as well as the 3/5th's of a human to create legislation for their ill way of thought. It reminds us of the burnings at the stake and the ritualistic character of it and the reality of 'Pic-a-Nigger' and the 'Barbeque'. In other words, a system was created to validate and vindicate their psychopathic and ritualistic behavior. He is simply a product of his ancestor's culture that has been passed down generation to generation. A psychopath feels no remorse or guilt as we can see in this situation. He actually blames the victims or what he sees as the stereotyped culture of the victims when confronted about his overtly undeniable racist behavior.

The greater issue is Amerikkkan culture and who dictates this culture, not Don Imus. The obvious answer is white Amerikkka, who also controls the corporate structure. I'm referring to radio, television and the system (Global White Supremacy) itself. This culture co-opts and distorts all other cultures they colonize and claim to embrace and integrate. This is what mainstream Hip-Hop has become, a bitch for Amerikkkan culture to use as a scapegoat as they impose the sickness of Amerikkkan culture. Some Hip-Hop has become the beast that this society nurtured with its insanity and capitalistic nature. With this being stated, how could Amerikkka ever deal with the historical and present guilt and truth of white supremacy whether it's spoken or acted out? They've yet to determine that this culture is a sickness and probably never will. Of course, many of the wards of this victimization have recognized this consciousness since coming in contact with Europeans even prior to Amerikkka. *See KMT as an example.* This society can't continue to talk about the problems, but ignore the cause of these problems. There is a cancer and it is causing other issues in the entire body, which means other parts of the body that was once very healthy becomes ill. White Amerikkka doesn't want to deal with that cancer (which is themselves), their culture and how the cancer within their culture and *spirit* attacks all that's normal and civilized in their surroundings. Everything and everyone else is a byproduct of that culture. We can't dialogue about the entertainment industry and not

19

talk about the corporate structure; it would be the C.E.O. of the label or whatever other titles given in corporate Amerikkka. Slaves to a system never want to blame 'masta' for the conditions created for them. He/she would rather blame the other slaves. This is how sick we've become by allowing foreign cultures to rule our minds and spirit. We'll fight amongst ourselves and blame each other for the problems that stem from White Supremacy and a white elitist culture. Does the person being raped blame the rapist or themselves? So what if it is 3a.m in the morning and you're in a dark alley. That doesn't mean the rapist still shouldn't be dealt with any less severely. It's the rapist that is the psychopath. As a people we have become as sick as the rapist. We weren't always this way but Amerikkkan culture or European culture in general always has been! What I'm saying to you is we have the capacity to change and they don't…at least not as a people or culture according to history!

White oppression has historically proven that it will not take the blame for social conditions created by white oppression. The oppressor then constructs a system to teach through education and mass propaganda that the victims of these conditions are the reason for the conditions and create the climate for their innocence and the victim's guilt. The victim should take responsibility for their actions if perpetuating these conditions but never allow the victimizer to not take responsibility for their invention of the racial and social conditions and barriers that are institutional and ongoing. Don Imus is the perfect example in 2007. It doesn't seem much different from 1807, but what's important is the fact that he initially didn't have a problem with the conversation over the airwaves. It was okay until disgruntled people told him it was out of line and asinine. Once major corporations pulled their sponsorships, Imus was fired for economic reasons, not moral or because of being racist. This is the mindset that isn't discussed by mainstream Amerikkka, especially white Amerikkka. I wonder how would white Amerikkka or Amerikkka in general feel if two black commercial personalities called white women basketball players straight-haired, white trash bitches or hoes? A racist psychopathic society determine and define the worth of its victims (all people of color) that creates worthlessness in our Afrikan (black) women from a standpoint of the system, society in general and the women themselves. As long as

Uncensored!

this psychopathic culture exists...a Don Imus will continue to exist and Amerikkkan culture will continue to make excuses to justify their mental sickness!

Europeans have crippled Afrikans to the point where
We depend on their crutches
Revolutionary Afrikans are the therapist
Who can show Afrikans that they can walk
Without the pale man's crutches, religion, ideologies, etc.

Imhotep Musa-Kushan

Interview

Uncensored!

Okera Damani is a Tajedi ("Griot"). He is a steward in the community and an excellent example of heritage, culture and leadership for the hip hop generation. When I first met Okera some years ago he was working with so-called at-risk youth and many of the well-respected elders in the community in regards to combating many of our social issues imposed by the oppressive state. This is an interview I did with him in the spring of '07.

Sadiki: *Why do you feel this Gestapo cowboy government co-opted, distorted, outright bastardized and colonized ancient Nile Valley civilization?*

Okera: They of course don't have, nor have ever had anything of substance in their own short geographical/political history to stand upon. Like all other non-Afrikans who had any contact with Northeast Afrikans since about the 3rd century B.C.E., they were astonished, dwarfed, amazed, jealous and envious of what they saw, heard of and experienced in their dealings with our ancestors. The three thousand-year legacy of Dynastic unifying upper and lower Kemet is the only and the most accessible documented example of a thriving, long lived civilization that had the respect, if not the outright worship from the rest of the world. No other civilization in antiquity can claim that type of influence and longevity including the already dying bully, misnomer, United States of America, born into existence in 1776 A.D. or more literally in 1863 after the civil war which "united" the northern union with the southern confederacy. The vast historical omission and distortion of Afrikan peoples' contribution was necessary to keep the lid on the biggest contradiction of those times; the genocide, capture, rape, destruction of and chattel enslavement of the very descendants of the Nile Valley, in a new world of supposed freedom from tyranny for all men.

Black Kemet was buried so that "Egypt" could have a life in the minds of the unaware. History became a well guarded, hidden secret of the select and elect; those who could stomach and/or profit off of the polished lies that masked the ugly truth of it. Nile Valley

Uncensored!

civilization was being attempted, at least in symbol and structure by the European masons and shriners who were in charge of shaping this government. The substance of Nile Valley Civilization could never be a reality here, because it is the practice and the highest regard for doing Ma'at. Our ancestors already referred to the Tamahu, or whites, Greeks and other pale invaders at the time as *"Spiritually Retarded"* and "Children of Tumult", etc. No Western so-called civilization has ever been successful at achieving anything close to harmony, balance, order, reciprocity, righteousness, etc. It's been the exact opposite, which is why those of us who are either victims of them, or with them, are so messed up.

We often talk about images and false symbolism and how this shapes one's reality. Is there a direct assault by the media to attack our Afrikan children's perception of Kemet, history or blackness in general?

Yes, there has been an ongoing psychological attack utilizing the weapons of mass propaganda, images and repetitive false statements by not only the media, but by the church and the academic educational system. When something is shown on the television news, or on the Discovery channel, or in a textbook, religious document or newspaper, it is viewed by most as factual, or at least valid, reliable "information". For example, we are trained in school to think that the "corporate" news and the newspapers are the best sources of "unbiased", "fair and balanced" investigative research and reporting on current affairs that we can trust. We are trained in church and in Sunday school to believe that the stories, events and personalities written of in the Bible and in biblical commentaries actually have real historical reference. We are also trained to label any other sources of information that contradict or challenge the mainstream prescribed ones as radical, extreme, hate-speech, conspiracy theory, lies, satanic, blasphemy, etc.

One has only to reflect back on the many negative, false, and disrespectful stories and images of Afrikans and Afrika, in cartoons, sitcoms, movies, commercial advertisements, documentaries,

Sunday services and bible school, and in the news. The catch is, one has to search for, find, study, and know the truth of our Afrikan ancestral heavily documented side of the story before he/she will have the ability to discern and confirm raw, organic facts from refined, processed fiction. If not, we would all still ignorantly hate ancient Afrikan Egypt, or *Kemet,* if we left it to what we have seen in movies like "The Prince of Egypt", "Stargate", and "The Mummy". We have been indoctrinated by the church about the so-called "evil pharaohs and the plagues and curses", etc., or what has been left out of scholastic history, math and science books and attributed to Greeks and other Europeans in post-colonial academia.

How has the images of white Deities and religion enslaved the spirit of Afrikans in the Diasporas?

When a people don't see, project and portray divinity in themselves on every level, including the physical, its clear evidence that they are not free or sane. We know that someone else has forcibly altered their perception on both conscious and subconscious levels. Afrikan people are the custodians of the concepts of spirituality, ethics, morality, cultural rituals and sacred ceremonies, and literary scriptures in stone, on sarcophaguses and on papyrus reed scrolls; which later became key components of *"religions"* for invading usurpers to conquer and control others with. When we can only see divinity in our oppressors and enslavers who have mostly acted in direct contradiction to the lofty idealisms in plagiarized "holy" texts, which is an even bigger sign of our immense collective ignorance and subsequent bitter hatred of ourselves through social, political, economic and especially religious conditioning. In antiquity, the closer one's skin tone was to the color black, the closer they were perceived by others to have embodied the most favorable attributes of the divine, NTR, nature all over the world which was mostly painted and portrayed as "jet black", like Amen, Auset, Ausaru, Ptah, Hathor, Krishna and Christ. Most people of Afrikan descent, who now consider these sacred, modern pink, pale pictures of the deities they worship like Mary and Jesus, know nothing about that. Think about that in the scope of this ongoing destructive aftermath

26

Uncensored!

of what is in my opinion the most successful culmination of a European religious and media propaganda campaign in history; the commissioning of *Michelangelo in 1505 A.D. by Pope Julius II*, to paint God in the image of a white man on the inner ceiling of the Sistine chapel in Rome.

Religion is really watered down, bastardized spirituality, trapped in its own scope of time, region and culture. It is the deification of the cultural norms of whoever forced it into circulation and acceptance through genocide, torture, rape, theft and years of alien occupation and oppression of the indigenous people. It's like cooked vegetables, stripped of its most vital nourishing essence once adapted to fit the control module it was created for. It's no accident that in every major world religious system, those with the darkest skin tend to be the least important and empowered; at the bottom. You are only on top when you are the conceiver, author, creator, engineer, evolver, editor and manipulator of whatever system that exists, period. The evidence of white idolatry exists in the majority of black churches in this country, as well as in Afrika, even in Ethiopia, Nigeria and Ghana. All one has to do is look up at the walls and stained glass windows, or in the pictorial bibles and Sunday school literature to find the glaring contradictions to historical, geographical and cultural awareness and relativity. The fact is that for most of us whose parents were very active in church while we were babies and children, got our first dose of *institutionalized anti-Afrikanism and self-hatred* in the same *"house of God"* that was supposed to be the source of our spiritual salvation.

You are one of the youngest Tajedi's and Griots that the torch has been passed to. What is the psychological and spiritual importance of preserving our history, not only for the hip-hop generation but for future generations to come?

Great question! Being that Tajedi means "teacher" and a Griot is one who keeps the story of a people alive and passing it down to younger generations is a great honor and responsibility to be identified as such. I have studied and continue to study the

27

awesome, in-depth research and literary/audio visual works of our revolutionary luminaries and masters such as Dr. John Henrik Clarke, Dr. Yosef ben Jochannan, Cheikh Anta Diop, Rev. Ishakamusa Barashango, Chancellor Williams, John G. Jackson, Dr. Khallid Abdul Muhammad, George G.M. James, Anthony Browder, Dr. Francis Cress-Welsing, Dr. Suzar, Bro. Nur Ankh Amen, Carol T. Barnes, Walter Williams, Dr. Ivan Van Sertima, Amos Wilson, Rev. Phil Valentine, Bro. Mathu Ater, Runoko Rashidi, Bro. Ashra and Sis. Merira Kwesi, as well as many others. I mentioned those names because they have had the most vital, potent and personal impact upon my Afrikan spiritual consciousness and development.

Without the knowledge of our ancient Afrikan history and heritage, we have no base, no basis, no foundation and no central connection to stand on psychologically or spiritually. This special, seemingly secret and highly sensitive data is the missing link, the un-deciphered code to the combination and the ripped out page to the roadmap of our success and survival as a group. As a general rule, anything that our enemies, colonizers and oppressors would go to such great, elaborate, expensive and extensive lengths to hide, destroy, and/or plagiarize and take credit for must be of significant value to us. On the other hand, anything that these same groups of enslavers and exploiters would willingly and openly share with us, or force upon us must be of significant value to them.

In the western world, the true accounts of Afrika and Afrikans in antiquity are the most widely unknown, suppressed and lied about, compared to any other subject matter including UFOs and so-called aliens. We are starting to connect the dots now. The time is right cosmically. This is the age of information. This is the new movement, real research, study and heightened knowledge of self outside of the maniacal myths and cultural constraints of religion. The hip-hop generation and all that follow are charged with advancing this inner movement of the mind until our collective consciousness crystallizes into massive actions that will empower us to put ourselves and this planet back in natural divine balance, as only we know how. We gave this planet balance, then it was

28

Uncensored!

destroyed and only we can bring it back once enough of us realize who we are, what we have done, and what we can and must do. Hotep.

MAAT HOTEP!

THE WORD!

Afro We

Face painted like Aborigine
Sultry n her Kush mid-drift
Matrilineal mother
Musical matriarch
Eons of prudent beauty
She rain danced long before Indian
He mapped out stars/ then taught the Mayans
She cuddles Mercury
He bathes Neptune
Designers of the universe
Prognosticator of time
Messiah of the Masai
Curled eyelash of slanted eye
Fore parent to Maat
Jiggle n her Bantu back
We be the first 2 sage, sage
Her afro nectar humble
Freedom strut
Somali rhythm hoofs n her switch
She transcends bitch
Up jump n satin blues boogie
She dips side 2 side
Sea Gypsy afro dance inside soul
Get up and get down
Leimert Park scribe
He be documenter of time
We b the original
Cousin 2 the Tang
Parents of the Mayas
Teacher to Mali
Lived infinite degrees of masonry
First to write on papyri
Cotton dashiki top counsels enslaved hip-hop
We make love inside the metaphysical
Her presence b an unwrapped present
Daughter of heaven's DNA

Original roller of the scroll
We defined and define
Humanity
Nurturer of the Dogon
Sculpturer of the Akan
They b the oral tradition of the original Holy land
For Mecca to listen to
Afro her and afro I, b afro we
We cha cha on invisible moonbeam
She b the motha of nappy
Replica of Ra
Night time primordial moon
Sister of Yoruba
God mother to O'shun
He be father of O' gun
Night stick that plant seed of tomorrow
Our afro timeless like before pole shifts
Continental drifts, b modern to us
Lion roar like our rhythm
I stroke her cosmic positions
All 360 of them…24/7
The first 2 c their savior in the mirror
I am God and she is Goddess
Long before definition
Transcending all interpretation
Shadows are simultaneous
Our shadows make love n sacred temple
Secret morning strokes
The breath of prophets
Spinner of the Potters wheel
I lick the seed of her melanin
She sings n the midst of triple blackness
First twister of the lock
Antenna to the source
We give birth to afros/ and she breastfeeds naps
Inside the womb of the universe
As energy spirals n her constant embryo
We procreate
Messiahs

Revolution

Revolution is not to rearrange
Revolution is complete change
Revolution is plot
Plan
Protocol
Strategy
Organization
Action
About more than black power buttons
Or who got the biggest Ankh
Or who got on the most red, black and green
Revolution is pepper spray
Possibly being part of your day
A flashlight to yo' windpipe
Dogs biting at yo' crotch
Jail time for no crime
24 hr. surveillance
Mispropaganda
Rumors
Lies
Revolution is ride or die
Maybe even both
Be willing to take up arms
The will to get in the way of harm
Revolution is saying
FUCK THE STATUS QUO
We against the status quo
Revolution is physical
Psychological
And spiritual

Revolution is now
Revolution is Mau Mau
Revolution is suicide bomber

Revolution is militia training
Revolution is sustaining
Revolution is Watts 1965
Revolution is Cuba and Venezuela
Revolution is Ethiopia
Battle of Algiers
Haiti
Angola
NAT TURNER
Insurrection
Revolution was and is field nigga
Revolution means yo'ass may never come home

Revolution is gas masks and box cutters
Pipe bombs
Car bombs
Revolution is fire fights
Revolution is 4 year old Palestinians
Throwing rocks at Israelis
Revolution is toppling the system
Changing the lives of yo' children's children
Lives that ain't even been born yet
Change that you ain't even seen yet
Revolution is that bomb you make
That bullet you might take
That new reality you create
Revolution is snipers on roof tops
PIGS getting shot
Most things in REVOLUTION
Ain't even talked about
Revolution is FRED HAMPTON
WILLIE RICKS MUKASA
PAM AFRIKA
Revolution is being in touch with yo' chakras
Revolution is identifying who and what is your enemy

Revolution says fuck Bratton
We ain't marchin'

We plottin'
We scheming
Revolution is not being enslaved by yo' own demons
Can you survive the jungle?
Can you remain humble?
Revolution is either you die or win
You damn sure gone lose a friend
Revolution is carrying out the mission
Without question

Revolution is freedom
Revolution is sovereignty
Revolution is liberation
Revolution is repatriation
Revolution is reparation
Transformation
Evolution
Retribution
Creativity
Reality
Revolution is the Ka
The Ba
The SitRA
The SaRA
The Sahu
Revolution is beyond me and you
Revolution is words that compel
Heaven vs. Hell
Revolution is transmigration of the soul
Revolution is metaphysical
Revolution is quantum
Matter vs. Anti-matter
Revolution is spirit
Soul
Energy
Passion
Phenomena
Revolution is pro-active

Not reaction
Revolution is cosmology

Revolution is bullet wound
Kill or be killed
Stalk or be stalked
Revolution is not reform
Revolution is not the norm
Revolution is grassroot, grimy and gritty
Revolution is guerrilla
Revolution is bold and bodacious
Revolution is vicious
Revolution is cautious
Revolution means all things have been exhausted
Revolution is socialist
Egalitarianist
Revolution is not racism
Fascism
Imperialism
Colonialism
Capitalism
Not authoritarianist
Totalitarianist
Not oppression
Repression
Suppression
Downpression
Dehumanization or degradation
Revolution is not an election
Not witness protection
Revolution is not compromise
Revolution is take action now
Ask questions later
Revolution means yo' ass will never take me alive
REVOLUTION!

Uncensored!

Liberation Song

She is my liberation song
She is Coretta Scott King as a queen
Reincarnated and personified
She is Harriet Tubman
Left her husband for freedom
She is Betty Shabazz standing next to Malcolm
She is Amy to Marcus Garvey
She is the woman that refused 2 give up her seat
Before Rosa Parks
She is Rosa Parks
She is the original trail of tears before ameriKKKa
Her sway is more than yo' eyes lusting for her hips
She is more than another rendition of a video vixen
Her truest essence be cosmic
When u treat her like a Goddess
U can leave yo' imprint on her uterus
The core of her innocence
She is the reason for the zodiac
Her womb represents wisdom
Her femininity parallels universes
Beyond 5 senses and scripture
She is revolution like conception
U can't put shackles on her afro
I love how she kisses my DNA
She is a metaphor like this poem
She is the womb of tomorrow, today
Ain't no propaganda n her moans
Ain't no fork tongue when she cums
Melanin be her sun tan
It's biological
She is prophecy unknown/ yet known
Heard but unheard
Her genetic memory bank is like red candy apple licks
The Holy Grail is the blueprint of her cells
She still calls the government gangstas

Uncensored!

Her locks massages aura
Her mannerism mimes ankhs
She timeless
Ancient like antique
Afrika still n the arch of her feet
Raw rhythm n her life cycle
She is sweet molasses like segregated Alabama
She is the manifestation of Asar and Auset's procreation's Karma
She only ask that u be consistent
Our Antique sista is metaphysical
Our existence together is quantum and dimensional
I insert my sunray n yo' Milky way
Black Power n the thrust
Dark skin is a must
She is insurrection never talked about
Nat Turner n the feminine
No mo oppression
The definition of freedom,
so I pray 2 her and never a white Jesus
I love her conversation cause her tongue stay nappy
She was the beauty of the Black Panther Party
She ain't picken nat cotton no mo
Black glove on right fist
She said Uncle Sam ain't her uncle
It's the back of her nipples that nurtured humanity
Only to be given the gift of patriarchy and misogyny
Her mystique is sanctified wit sacred sacrifice
She speak n tongues when she meditates
She already scribed what is now rewritten
She is before Asian made Kente'
Euro "peon"
Asiatic black man
Christianity
Catholicism
Judaism
Islam
All religion
She births spirit
She transcends Dashiki tops and head wraps

Uncensored!

U won't find her n a feminist movement
She is the antithesis and genesis of every culture's story
Greece, Rome and Arabs could only mimic her poorly
She is the reason this poems exists
She is lips to kiss
This is her liberation song
And she is the best poem ever written

Uncensored!

Sankofa

Haitian revolution
Metaphysical
Voldun
Fuck Schwerner and Goodman
Evil spirits
Backwoods of Mississippi
Backward
Southern cotton fields
Slaves for sale
Washington D.C
Barter for the buckest nigga
Sellouts
Auction block @ poetry venue
Sellout the insurrection
Uncle Tom wasn't a tom
Emancipation Proclamation
Please
Why do we still celebrate Juneteenth
Slavery is still legislation
Niggers was livestock
Bred and raised cattle
Hue-mans seen as animals by animals
Sun up to sundown
Moonshine porches
Backwoods
Pork dinner
Outhouse
Tobacco spittin' racist
Barbaric culture
Inferiority complex
Considered themselves businessmen
Spoke n redneck slang
Raped our Goddess
Miscegenation

Uncensored!

Assassination
Crucified primordial man
Black messiah
Ascend
Broken family and spirit
Stolen culture and land
Desecration
Cut out Griot tongue
Illiteracy
Slavery n the form of religion
Spiritual disenfranchisement
Live portraits of flog marks
Cross burnings
Burnings @ the stake
Confederate flag
Traditions for the next generation
Rituals
Belief systems
Senators and congressmen
Crooked politician
Pimp hat mistaken for top hat
Genetics
Blue eyes
Indignant spirit
Deviant
First Caucasian to white ameriKKKan
Fork tongue said Indian
Goree Island
Elmina Castle
Gold Coast
Slave ship
Christian hypnosis
Malnutrition
Follow the big dipper
Wait n na water
Dehydration
Middle fuckin' passage
Middle fuckin' finga

Universal language
West Indies slave breaking grounds
Couldn't break us
Broke us
Sacred
Secret
Liberation song
Long
Still singin'
Libation
Rosewood
Slave narratives
Bloodhounds
Underground
Railroad
Harriet
No reparation
No repatriation
Garvey
Afrika for Afrikans
Kushite Ethiopian
South Afrikan Apartheid
Soweto Townships
Free labor still
Neo-cons con neo-phites plight
Fire holes and protest
Black power
Industrial prison complex
Neo-Nazi
Prison segregation
Willie Lynch for Blacks and Mexicans
Fight each other
Instead of the system
Psychological prison
Psychoanalyzed us
3 strikes law
Gang injunctions
White man's law

Uncensored!

Nihilism
Poverty
Class system
Modernized systemic oppression
Bootlicka
Petty Negro bourgeoisie
Shuck and jive
New form of sambo
Brown nosin', butlickin', ass kissin'
Niggaz
Fuck patriots
Still minstrel
Watermelon
Equal rights
Wrong fight
Black Wall Street
Self-determination
Black fist
Afro-pick
Origin of Kwanza
Afrika
Free' em all
Integration
Mistake
Assimilation
Same mistake
Illusion of acceptance
House nigga
Same plantation
Corporate AmeriKKKa
Mothafucka
SANKOFA!

"First and Foremost, WE ARE AFRICANS!!!
We MUST
Do for ourselves and thoroughly know
Our history and culture
In order for us to be liberated
In any shape, form or fashion
That's the TRUE meaning of SANKOFA
As an African people, our strength is spirituality
Spirit is beyond the physical realm (metaphysical)
Once we tap back into our inner-self (inner-gy)
We'll be FREE!!!"

Bro. Tessema G.

Nigga Please

How we gone be a revolutionary
But can't wait for the cameras to come on
Got every media channel on speed dial
No longer underground
Since when is violence not an option
They want reform not revolution
Want press and accolade
What happened to counterterrorism
They ain't nothing but exploiters
Capitalist
Opportunist
Trying to appeal to the ignorant masses
They wearing suit and ties
Wit strong rhetoric as camouflage
Talk revolution and then exploit it
Sit at the table begging
Pleading and compromising
Got contracts with the government
Lending credibility to the system within

I'm Amerikkkan
Vote democratic
Fight for multicultural studies
Try to fit in
Get yo' degree
Wait for Jesus
That's reverse racism
Not all white people are racist
Why would you want to be sovereign?
What about John Brown
Integration
Diversity
We all free now
Slavery is over

Reform
Conform
Embrace everyone
You are a conspiracy theorist
We all equal

My Gods better than your God
Pathological racism doesn't exist
Genocide doesn't exist
Institutionalism doesn't exist
Germ warfare doesn't exist
Profiling doesn't exist
Stereotypes doesn't exist
Class-ism doesn't exist
What's a political prisoner?
Revolutionaries are enemy combatants
Mind control is a conspiracy theory
Thugs killed 2Pac and Biggie not the government
Prop 209 was reverse discrimination
We need 3 strikes for criminals not rehabilitation
My Lord and savior Jesus Christ
We send aid to 3rd world countries
Don't forget to support the troops
We got civil liberties and civil rights
They wouldn't change the laws
The Black Panthers were radicals
We support Homeland Security,
The Patriots Act and the Terrorist Bill
Black people loot
White people find
We believe in the National Guard
White collar crime
Wouldn't take 1 penny
Out of every citizen bank account daily
Government is doing the best they can
We still building Afghanistan
It takes time to get aid to those refugees
We need more money for weapons

48
Uncensored!

Send airlift units to the suburbs first

What happened to I'm Afrikan
Pan Afrikanism
Nationalism
Fuck multiculturalism
Fuck the police
I'm taking my reparations
Slavery has only changed forms
They criminalize us
White people are barbaric
Ain't no man named Jesus ever coming back
No conformity
Revolution not reform
Don't trust white folk or the government
No passes for Bill Cosby
No mo religious gang bangin'
Pimpin' or exploitation
Reverse racism can't exist
Create our own reality
Fuck the law and the con-stitution
Take sovereignty
Free the land
Free the people
Free the minds and spirit of the people
Free the political prisoners
The government is terrorists
Uncle Sam ain't my uncle

The Trade Center should've been blown up along time ago
Dirty money can't stay clean forever
Bring disorder to new old world order
Counterterrorism for police terrorism
Send Europeans back to their caves on ships
New cointelpro killed Pac and Biggie
Villaraigosa is a white boy wit a taco
Amerikkka steals the resources from Afrika

Uncensored!

Ain't no refugees misplaced from New Orleans
We don't support Homeland Security
Patriot Acts
Land Grab
Bullshit elections
Iraqi Freedom means Iraqi slavery
Why didn't the government respond to
Cuba and Venezuela's offer of aid for Hurricane Katrina
Since when have we become refugees?
Why weren't the levees fixed?
Why did the military bomb the levees?
Why are these niggaz still religious?
Why do they think religion is spirituality?
Why do niggaz think knowledge is belief or faith?
Because that's what yo' oppressor taught you
And you have yet to teach yourself
Global white supremacy is institution

Uncensored!

Ashe' for Shay ☺

Sweet honey libation lips
Soft like unexplainable
Tip of tongues touch
Til spirit cum
Tight love nest
Wet wit mystic opium aura

Rhyme n the abode of yo' antique moonshine
Long legs of aged infinity
U r the hindsight of my future thrust
Constant rhythm n the wisdom of yo' womb
I am consumed by yo' karma
I want 2 trace yo' curvature
Fingertips fondling yo' sway

My ancient tongue
Caress yo' indigenous moan
We meditate togetha
Electromagnetic ohm

Yo' fallopian tube is nature
Yo' uterus is nurture
Yo' lips loves like the forever
Mandingo pays homage to U
When planting seed of life inside U

Sweet honey libation lips
Sweet like morning molasses
Ancient like first born
Timeless like far as can remember
I am humbled by the antiquity of yo' genes

"It takes a woman to know how to be a woman,
just like it takes a man to know how to be a man.
A woman doesn't know what manhood feels like,
and a man sure can't give birth.
So, to say that God is only a man
is to also deny a woman's worth."

Shay Fresh

Homage

This poem pays homage to revolution
For Ya Asantewa
Who were ready 2 shed blood
For every Ashanti warrior that took arms with her
For Harriet Tubman
Who put guns 2 house niggaz heads
For every train that made it
Every slave that didn't
Every guerrilla militant executed n the high mountain
Every plan that was successful
For the plan that failed
Those that were jailed
Those subject to chemical warfare
Mind control
Those who were drugged
Those that were hung
Those who jumped of ships
Those with unbroken spirit
For those that were tortured
Those who fought till death
Embraced last breath
Those unnamable
Unidentifiable
Those who sacrificed limb and phlegm
For every field nigga that infiltrated the house
and put glass n masta's grits
Every sista that called masta's wife a bitch
Every Afrikan that plan and plotted insurrection
For NAT TURNER
HARRIET TUBMAN
GABRIEL PROSSER
TOUSSAINT L' OUVERTURE
DENMARK VESEY
DAVID WALKER

SAM SHARPE
PAUL BOGLE
JEAN DESSALINES
MANGALISO SOBUKWE
For those not mentioned
For every slave on na chain gang that escaped
Every slave that refused 2 be raped
Every slave that refused 2 be whipped
Those who refused 2 get on the ship
For every Essene that refused 2 accept
Euro "peon" religion
Every victim of police terrorism
This poem is for cointelpro assassinated victims
FRED HAMPTON
SANDRA "RED" PRATT
BUNCHY CARTER and JOHN HUGGINS
MARK CLARK
BRENDA HARRIS
GEORGE JACKSON
JONATHAN JACKSON
KING
X
For those not mentioned
For those the government didn't get
Those who lived n the bush for freedom
Those who knew they needed someone
2 lead them
This poem is for Haiti
HANNIBUL
NZINGA
SORJOURNER
PATRICE LUMUMBA
RWANDA
For every Essene who took back his scroll
Every revolutionary who shot back at cointelpro
For those who gave their babies guns
For the Afrikans that still fight
Palestinians that still fight

Iraqis that still fight
So-called Dalits that still fight
Aborigines that still fight
West Papuans that still fight
For every sista that nurtured the movement
We pay homage 2 every grassroots movement
Documented
Undocumented
Named
Unnamed
Titled or untitled
For the cotton that wasn't picked
Every brotha who killed a snitch
For those Afrikans with the big noses and big lips
For those that didn't survive the trip
This poem is for Black Nationalists
Pan Afrikanists
Socialists
For HATSHEPSUT
KWAME NKRUMA
KWAME TURE'
SEMURE TURE'
SNCC
BLA
BPP
REPUBLIC OF NEW AFRIKA
U.N.I.A
The organizations not mentioned
For every bullet fired
Every slit throat
Every neck broke
Every new hope
For that silent brotha who finally spoke
For every suicide mission
Every suicide bomber
For revolutionaries n the diasporas
Those faced with freedom
Those faced with oppression

Those faced with persecution
We love u and honor u
This poem pays homage 2 revolution
Those named and unnamed!

Responsible

Historically wicked
Vile
Shitted n Nile
Pedophilia
Corporate slave mastas
No diplomacy
New world plantation
No regret
Ignorant
Responsible for
Regret
Neglect
Invention of Super Nigga
Slavery
Post and modern
Poverty
9 to 5
Skid Row or food stamp
Equality is an illusion
Trying 2 forward reverse discrimination
Adjacent mirror
Tight white rope
Conservative coalition
Neo-right wing
Backwards left-ism
Equality n reverse
Illusion rehearsed
Personified
Inferiority complex
Sleeps with superiority complex
Invisible rusted chain stain seat of upliftment
Slave auction mentality
White chain of command
Reprimand freedom

Uncensored!

False sense of self
Acculturation
Responsible for contraband
Terrorism
Is yo last name Afrikan
Cops profiling me
Billy Club parties in Compton and why the fuck they call it Billy
U look nervous
Reasonable cause
Suspicion
U fit the description
K-9's sniffin' me
Prejudice
Racism
Manifestation of reality
Irresponsible
Only I am responsible for
REVOLUTION
Combat training
Activation of melanin
Retribution
Hieroglyphic n blood
Change
Rotted roots
Meditation
Healed
Healthy from riot and rise
Cleanse
Soul transmigration
Generation of new song
Ancient spirit
Reparation and then Repatriation
Part of the solution
Still not enough
The afterbirth
Liberation
Who will b responsible?
R U?

Uncensored!

Untitled

Eyes like the inside of the sun
U
Shine on melanin
We bask in sun ray
Consumed by yesterday
Just the thought of u
Tickles soul's esteem

Cradler of Shango
Generator of heat
Hug like inside of blanket
When did u fall n love
With the thought of love

I fondle time 4 u
Just 2 give us more moments, together
Moments become mementos
Keepsakes in future
We c the unpredictable
Master the predictable
As my 3rd eye opens yours
U didn't know that I'm really yo' first
Ask my stroke if it honors u
As u embrace truth
I lick yo' aura
U
Will never experience anyone like me
And I u
Foreplay n the spiritual
Orgasms n the metaphysical
We moonwalk and hold hands

We r like Abraham and Sarah
Jacob and Leah
The sun and the moon

59
Uncensored!

Saturn's babies
Babies of O' Shun
Niece of Venus
Godson to Neptune

Together n a prior life
We love like SANKOFA
Walked the ancient Sahara
Wiped the trail of tears
Looked back at Djoser
Imhotep recited our poems

Our love is so deep
Its title is untitled
The spiritual realm has a cosmic sanctuary
Waiting for us
Transmigration of the soul can't wait to c us
We are free!

Uncensored!

Man Sway

Man is too busy trying to put makeup on his flaws
Ass on his shoulders
Stupidity on his mind
Arms folded
Hands on his hips
I see through the insanity
It greets me with crooked smiles
They frown in your mind when u revolt
They only want your vote
Our names have been edged in slave blood
History have been reincarnated
In the ridges of slipknots
Slipknots that don't take naps
We sleep in dreams of solutions
Awaking to reality's problems
We've been terrorized by police in reincarnation
A black rose scorned
Rising to incarceration
A bounty on our spirit
Possessed by evil spirits
We are imprisoned by a snow white mentality
Even Disney depicts racism
Imprisoned by 9 to 5's
Computers
Media outlets
False sense of time
Materialism
We are the offspring of secular mentalities
Although we are the valedictorians of life
Did you not know this?
Why are our lives validated by the insane?
Irrational instability
Sulks in the right side of our brain
The left side is not rational

Who is really speaking?
Our soul is not ripe
Diluted by fiction
Our resurrections have been illustrated as illusions
We gnaw at tomorrow
Villages never had street signs, or did they?
Are we confused?
We hear less and see less
Know less and believe more
We are less than abnormal
That makes us abnormal
We mimic barbarians
Our hair is not full
Depressed from being pressed
We dance in holy spirit and think it's Christianity
We've yet to tell religion we are not free
We can't see over the mountain top
Can't see past our eyelids
Stuck in the Europeanism of hip-hop
What is religion and how does it pertain to us?
When will spirituality snatch us out of religious slavery?
If white is perceived as beautiful then what are we?
Perception is persuasion
Simple conformity
Social rearing
We are a closed-caption people
You don't understand them or me

Timeless

Write 2 be timeless
Write words that aren't wordless
Write words that don't ask
But DEMAND
Scare folk like David Walker
Speak of violence
Speak of eye for an eye
Make threats like Al Qaeda
Threats like Castro
Bang on Bush like Hugo
Tongue be Oklahoma bombing on page
Thoughts kidnap conservatism for ransom
Analogies fight till death called Haitians
Words jump off cliffs like zealots
Be
Fire to kerosene skin
Line murdering lies like tech nine bullet
Perforate flesh
Be a sniper wit words and don't miss
Atomic energy n word be atomic bomb 2 system
Truth kills like mustard gas
Like mailed anthrax sealed
Truth be nuclear war 2 propaganda
This timeless poem dropping biological warfare on government
Penmanship be weaponry
Poems be military
Metaphors like BLACK FISTS n the 60's
Verbal sword ready 2 cut enemy's tongue
Make timeless poems that bitch slap the power structure
Be timeless like the unknown
Write shit so powerful
It'll get u killed
Shit so powerful
It'll make u live

Timeless words that start movements

Lines that
RIDE
RIOT
RISE
STRIVE
UPLIFT
SHOOT
KILL
STEAL
STEAL BACK WHAT WAS STOLE

Similes that piss off
Lines that piss on
Spit on
AmeriKKKan and confederate flag
Poems that shoot at Uncle Sam's hat
Poems that damn sho will shoot back
Write hyper hyperboles
Write monologues that force dialogue
Theatrical plays that don't play
Write about coups instead of haikus
Write solutions n code
No compromise
Lines that call people racist if necessary
Hypocrites if necessary
Faggots if necessary
Snitches if necessary
Must say it by any means necessary
Even if it means
Yo' car
Yo' house
Yo' spouse
Yo' job or even yo' life
Poets did that
Freedom fighters did that
So do that

Uncensored!

Yo' words have to
INSIGHT
IGNITE
EVOKE
PROVOKE
Dismantle media propaganda
Right to change, write to change
Write like sages
Like messiahs
Be prophets
Be evolution
Be revolution
Be manifestation
Right to reaffirm
Affirm
Confirm
Unrelenting tongue prophesizing tomorrow
Today
Writing still relevant thousands of years from now
Depicting the now
Powerful like tight nap
Right to kill isms
Write to kill isms
May yo' pen have sovereignty
Open doorways never seen
Write for the forever
WRITE RED, BLACK AND GREEN WORDS
That do drive-bys on red, white and blue words
BANG ON NA' SYSTEM!!!!

Uncensored!

"*Don't be disposable.*
Verb your art in a manner in which
It can live tomorrow without you."

Nikki Skies

Art

1st Amendment
Crucified resurrection
Not enough freedom
Comes wit conditions
Conditioned to be conditioned
Brown-nosin' manifestation of thought
Harlem Renaissance
Protest on paper
Claud McCay
If we must die
Published slave named Jupiter
Before boom box and Kangos
Remember Rap
Iman Jamil Abdullah Al-Amin
formerly H.Rap
Brown vs. Board of Education
Metaphors and analogies
No autonomy
Black Arts Movement
After New Negro
Untainted truth
True hip-hop
A long time ago
Broken down cardboard box n the middle of Crenshaw
Beatbox between rebellions
Hip-hop before it went pop
Jimmy Hendricks at Woodstock
Then came Hoodstock
Kinda ghetto
We'z coonin for dollars
So-called gangsta rap
Whatever happened to Watts Stax
Amiri Baraka
Who Blew Up AmeriKKKa

Tongue cut government
Uncompromising Poet Laureate
No mo' butt-lickin niggaz now
Memories inside her pen
June Jordan
Approach her approach
Literary competency
Words animate energy
Khallid Abdul Muhammad
Katrina poems
History under water
Mukasa Dada
Black Power
Kwame Ture
March on Washington
Not what you think
Marvin X
Black arts
Black Panthers
Huey P.
Nappy Tongue
Feed the People
Infinity
Kemetic war poem
Set the tone
Ancient literature
Disgruntled invasion
Sumerian
Dedication to Semerkhet
The children
Taught papyri and scroll
Chant and song
By original tongue
Phonetic
Music
Medicinal
Vibration
Healing through sound

Sonya Sanchez
Enough said
Nikki G.
Dedication to 2Pac
Gil Scott
Words for revolution
Askia Ture
Poem for Assata
Liberated political prisoner
Sista
Soja
Sista Soja on Donahue
Wordsmiths pass torch to next generation
Humility
Butt naked
Raw
Uncensored
Art
Must depict grisly
Savage and morbid
Insides of inhumanity
Personified
Vietnam
War poem and I told you so
Tenderloin Book Fair
Sam Greenlee
Guerrilla film-maker
The Spook
We uprocked to battle our inner battle
Resistance and Struggle
My first published article
Cleopatra Jones and Coffee
Ome Kongo
Welcome to the Congo
The drum
Niggaz are scared of revolution
The Last Poets, won't be last
Even Watts had Prophets

Greece had plagiarists
Rome too
Kushites
1st to write n cursive
So-called 70's exploitation flicks
Fly-away collar dress codes
Repatriated afros
Goodbye Uncle Tom and Sankofa
Slavery depiction
Roots
A movie
Birth of a nation
Crakkka please
That would be racism
Public enemy
WE STILL # 1

Articles!

War on Terror

Who will applaud this democratic republic wrongfully called a democracy? The war on terror is a farce. That would mean bullshit. The war is on freedom. The biggest threat for Afrikans or blacks isn't outside the United Snakes borders but inside these policed borders. This is the same government that votes on bills and legislation at 2 am in the morning when an uninformed nation is sleeping, 'literally'. This is the same government that discounts or doesn't count at all the votes of the people; not that it would matter anyway. Very few asked what was the relationship between the United Snakes government and Al Qaeda or Sadam Hussein? What happened to the weapons of mass destruction? Will they eventually say Iran or North Korea has terrorist cells in the U.S as if they planted their flags here like the U.S in Baghdad? Would MK Ultra be considered terrorism? This is and always has been an outlaw government since its inception. They spit on U.N "United Nations" policies and the United Nations ignores the illegal deployments and blatant war crimes by this regime. What ever happened to the illegal invasion and occupation in Afghanistan? The U.S hands are all in the asses of Darfur and Azania. We know that Arabs and Muslims are seen as the new niggaz being racially profiled and guilty until proven innocent for the moment anyway. Was the lynching policies excluded from terror by this government? Is chemical warfare like white phosphorous and cluster bombs on unarmed civilians not considered terror while anti-war protests goes on around the world?

The Government still seems to be carrying out Bush Sr. New World Order Speech although the concept wasn't new. The U.S bombing of Libya, Somalia and Sudan would be considered terror right. We wonder why people in AmeriKKKa dislike the system of AmeriKKKa and the people who facilitate it. We realize liberty isn't given. It is taken. Terror is police dogs biting the crotch of innocent civilians in the civil rights movement. What war did the government wage on that? This country celebrates the birthdays of known terrorists, rapists, and slave owners. This government is the greatest proponent of militarism and western capitalism. Are they not building McDonalds and other big businesses in Afghanistan? Remember, the war on poverty was the war on the people *in* poverty, wards of the oppressive state and the class system. In the midst of all of these bullshit operations are world hunger and sanctions on those that refuse to bow down to AmeriKKKan bravado and leadership of the true axis of evil. Why rape and sodomize the women and the babies? This would be a question for the military. How can an uncivilized country bring its inhumanity to other countries and claim to civilize them? To date at least 700 thousand innocent unarmed civilians have been killed in Iraq by U.S and British soldiers. How many Iraqi soldiers have killed so-called AmerKKKans here in the U.S? We revolt against police terrorism and racism in these dirty streets everyday. Now they consider us enemy combatants. This is a belligerent dictatorship. We're supposed to forget about slavery, biological and chemical warfare, Black Wall Street as well as cointelpro's assault on The Black Power and civil rights movements and Pine Ridge as well. The so-called Jews remind you of their holocaust every chance they get don't they? They never mention the Afrikans who were victims of that very same holocaust. I guess it's not terror if inflicted by the U.S while hue-mans in the diasporas starve. Israel is still receiving 90 percent of this government's foreign aid. Wouldn't that be <u>ECONOMIC TERRORISM</u>? Palestinians are being targeted indiscriminately by Israeli troops. Now the U.S is shitting in their pants since North Korea and Syria has nuclear capability. I'm sure there would never be a ground attack against North Korea. This government's ego is still molested and raped after the Vietnam fiasco.

Is anything worse than this government's response to Hurricane Katrina? The best example I can give is 200 million dollars was spent to renovate The New Orleans Superdome while millions of blacks (not refugees) were displaced wondering where their next meal would come from. I guess a professional sport is more important than black lives. Venezuela and Chavez offered 1 million dollars, 18 water purifiers, 20 tons of water, 50 tons of food, 2 medical supply ships and 18 power generators to the victims of Katrina. The United Snakes refused to accept it. Isn't that terror? What does that say about their feelings for blacks once again? Did

Uncensored!

you forget what Barbara Bush said? Didn't Halliburton receive the construction contracts? Would planted explosives be considered terror? How about the 4,000 so-called Jews that didn't show up for work at the trade centers on 9-11. That was surely swept under the rug by the heavily owned Jewish media. Did you forget the stocks taken out on Sept. 6th and 9th on United and American Airlines? Isn't all of this terror? There used to be a George Washington, then there was a Reagan and now there's a Bush all over again. This is why many people feel THE WAR ON TERROR is against the U.S but I guess this is the AmeriKKKan way. If this isn't Babylon then it's his little brother or maybe his illegitimate son. THE WAR IS ON FREEDOM. May yo' tongue stay nappy!

Educational Right Wing Terrorism

The oppressor has always used history to preserve their false inalienable right and reality of superiority whether it is historical colonialism or neocolonialism. Their inferiority complex is deeply rooted in the blatant westernized fixation with Greece's mimicking of ancient Afrikan civilization as well as the intellectual arrogance and masturbation in this Amerikkkan neo-ethnically cleansed system of programming and reprogramming that some relent to as education. We refer to it as neo-right wing mis-education and the education industrial complex which promotes illusions and unconsciousness for Afrikans. For the oppressed to be educated by his or her psychopathic, neurotic and habitual racist oppressor is insanity to say the least. They have colonized not only persons and history but nature, spirituality and even time. Greece, Rome, so-called Jews and western academia has truly earned a plagiarism degree in the many high sciences that they have bastardized.

A quote from astronomer Johannes Kepler states: "Nothing restrains me; it is my pleasure to taunt mortal men with the candid acknowledgement that I am stealing the golden vessels of the Egyptians to build a tabernacle to my God from them, far, far away from the boundaries of Egypt." This quote is from Book 5 in his series 'Harmony of the World'. They are incapable of self-actualizing spirituality. There is a very damaging force attacking our spirit, seat of the soul, genetic memory bank, reality, perception, and Afrikan center. This pathological behavior has been historically and systematically documented and proven by craKKKers themselves. Psychological Terrorism has been preserved and remanufactured in every aspect of Euro "peon" dogma. The impetus for higher knowledge is spiritual and moral innerstanding. When will we overstand that morals and values must be placed above human need, greed and worship of materialism? The magnificent historian Chancellor Williams stated, "The necessary re-education of blacks and possible solution of the racial crisis can begin…only when blacks fully realize this central fact to their lives: The white man is their bitter enemy."

Uncensored!

The pandemic educational system is a breeding and bleeding plantation for a more complex corporate plantation that some misinterpret as success in AmeriKKKa. The slave and master relationship still manifests itself in this construct. A neo-ethnically cleansed educational system forcing one to assimilate into a predominately capitalistic established and owned industrial business force due to covert bondage, servitude and slavery, of course is a grim reality accept for those who practice self-reliance and community. It's called unemployment and under-employment. Education is a major part of the robotism that exists in the Afrikan Diasporas. AmeriKKKan education is one of the hallmarks of Global White Supremacy. The public school system is a crime against our humanity. The deception of knowledge and information has been intensified by secret government intelligence agencies. Profound awareness has now been colonized by blatant oppressive propaganda. The originator of thought and manifestation is now imprisoned by their former malice students who impose their belief systems and theories on everything from education to spirituality. It's the essence and butt naked realization of imperialistic war mongers who misrepresent themselves as civil, humane and the authors of civilization and high science. They truly represent white hegemony, thievery, rape, molestation, corruption and inhumanity. These misfits have used our knowledge against us. Although misplaced in nature, they have been placed here for a reason. We must experience our lower nature to adorn ascending nature.

It will take rational thought from a true Afrikan center to dismantle this western fragmented paradigm of education to restore certain aspects of humanity. This paradigm is perpetuated by the lack of self knowledge, self hate, conditioning and skillful methodology that rejuvenates this system of white hegemony, racism, chauvinism, misogyny and capitalism in the educational system. Many of us have become patriots for the so-called intelligentsia. Slaves as oppose to creative and independent thinkers. Liberated thought is a nuisance to social rearing, social constructs and matrixes dependant upon distorted, misguided and confused mindset and vision. The curriculums are at the least anti-African and anti anything that promotes critical analysis. This anti-Kemetism exists in most of their history and school books as well as right wing philosophy controlling the curriculum while promoting multiculturalism, diversity and assimilation. This is an absolute contradiction. This elitism exists in the education of history in the many institutions of so called higher learning. There is a total destruction and dehumanization of Afrikan legacy in the diasporas as interpreted and misinterpreted by racist dogma, doctrine, belief, perception, ideology, theory, conjecture, supposition, hypothesis and philosophy, or whatever else is the basis for such undeniable lies in the genre of United Snakes colonial thought and imposed reality. The imposition of one's thoughts promotes colonization of mind, body and soul.

We often forget we are the authors of the trinity, art, alchemy, architecture, chemistry, biology, anatomy, agriculture, language, writing, cosmology, monotheism, psychology, philosophy, and that is a short list. We are more than just the cradle of civilization. We are the original mothers and fathers that created and nurtured it. This isn't an intellectual argument yet the argument still exists. This structural discrimination, racism and social rearing still exist in the colonizing paradigm of western thought whether it be education, history or any manifestation of it. Steven Biko stated, "The greatest weapon in the hands of the oppressor is the mind of the oppressed." Fuck this fascist, elitist, imperialist and totalitarian system of neo-right wing mis-education. May you think independently and may your tongue stay nappy!

The Secret Art of
Bloodless Murders

Modern penal practices here in the United States (particular emphasis is placed upon the racist repressive advanced technological industrial model state of California) are geared toward realizing the perfect *"Disciplinary Society"* totalitarianism. Behind the mist and mysteries of this vast criminal empire exists manifold projects that operate in their singular fields of activity; yet, they oppress themselves monolithically or as an organized whole that acts as a single unified power and force. In other words, U.S. jails and prisons are not singly money-making industries of legalized slave labor, or experimental labs of psychology, or pharmaceutics and marketable products, or public check and population control, or racist institutions that studiously breed human hatred and tendencies toward maniacal mentation, or pragmatic points of training in the dark art of surveillance and group infiltration of gangs, religious sects, etc; or toxic environments of human disease and rot – no! U.S. jails and prisons are actual models of what is envisioned and purposed over the whole range of the so-called *New World*.

Within these lawful and public-supported bedlams reign the *"Devil Supreme"* and its eerie array of grotesque creatures. The scenarios herein are always exceedingly barbaric and bizarre but in a way that is quite unspeakable because of the unseen mechanics of power and force. Most of the heartless and homicidal practices that are being perpetrated in this Dark Age are realized in *bloodless murder*. This *"Secret Art of Stealth Killing"* is so furtive and indirect, so imperceptible and sneaky that a lot of people cannot even conceive of this art actually being murdered by it. Accordingly, we do not count it as being a murder when one of us are mad-driven, poked and probed right out of our minds, our morals and our self-confidence to the tragic extent that the hope of a better future is altogether lost. It is not considered as being a murder when one of us is sentenced to life imprisonment on questionable findings and procedures or perceived as being a murder when a notable voice and vision of higher consciousness is isolated and silenced by a faithless and fickle network of jealousy, envy, greed, covetousness, fear,

79
Uncensored!

ignorance, vanity, racism, profanity and the popular culture of violence and 'getting high'. On the average, we are automatons – a deceived and defrauded people who have been acculturated and assimilated, (set in the wrong orientations) whereby we do not move on an original thought, but rather we thoughtlessly respond automatically to a set of encoded instructions and subtle suggestions. Subliminal messages. This will explain to some degree why we welter in such strong-holds of misery and wreck. *The Agents of Iblis* have predetermined our response to crisis situations and any marked deviation from the set of instructions will be immediately met by collective opposition. This too will explain to some degree, why we so grievously fail to readily see the *Secret Art of Bloodless Murder.* We have been so thoroughly trained, drilled and disciplined – locked into a set of pre-determined principles that will not allow freedom of thought and which cannot tolerate the "Creative Minds" of others. How then, is it possible for us to accurately comprehend the horrid things that are actually taking place behind the barbed-wire fences and up under the military assault rifles of U.S. prisons? In more ways than we know, Beloved Reader, we are just not capable of rightly communicating a lot of critical issues that affront and stab at us. Make no mistakes about it, effective communication and being accurate in the interpretations of the facts that are being communicated is a dreadful menace to the Modern Power. Wherefore, it is more than merely suggested that we live in strange lusts and lies - indeed! It is demanded, in both subtle and open points of import that we carefully cultivate all kinds of wild and elaborate fantasies of racial harmony, of societal stability and of economic opportunities according to one's abilities. This will also explain why one is liable to hear a prisoner, locked up by dirty tricks and legal language of esoteric purpose; condemn himself and his fellow inmates for their own choices in crime. It is never even hinted that there is something amiss about these strange state of affairs. But, the *Secret Art of Bloodless Murder* - this hard, ruthless rape of the souls of men, is no wise delimited to dust those who are ensnared in U.S. jails and prisons – for this unseen sprinkle of arsenic is cast upon the entirety of the so-called "Free Citizens" as well. Then, if we so happen to hear the frantic and half-intelligent shout of a prisoner who yells "Murder! Murder!", and we do not see

Uncensored!

a bloody and mutilated corpse, we automatically dismiss the messenger as being a fool who is perhaps a dite (bit) stir-crazy. More significantly if that prisoner so happens to be "Black", then we will ignore the message altogether.

But now as this *Secret Art of Bloodless Murder* is being daily practiced and sanctioned by human indifference, trauma, fear and ignorance, the death toll is astronomical and is increasing with such rapidity to where "Novus Ordo Seclorum" shall doubtless be established in a minute. But, I am seeing something these dark days – something that is quite hideous and that works an unearthly knack for confusion and contradictions. It is no doubt a curious thing to see – the dead raised and walking and talking by the witchery of cultural voodoo. What I am here saying (seeing) is that after the *Bloodless Murder* has been perpetrated, a cultural séance raises up armies of zombies – outright weirdoes who possess an uncanny skill in spiritual disturbances and distractions. These zombies were killed in different states of consciousness (some intelligent – some ignorant) where they are to be found amongst both the lofty and the lowly. The most marvelous of all mysteries here, however, is that these zombies are apt to show (if you can see it) a distinct pattern of deviltry. You would think that they belong to one of those satanic cults or Secret Luciferiarist orders (and some of them do, or at least they have been in some way, impressed by such dark arts) because of this distinct way of causing kerfuffles. Their most outstanding features of course - to foment discord and tension – to create chaos and dissension for the sole purpose of emotional disruption and inner turmoil. This is their playing field. The thing to remember here, Dear Reader, is that this is a dead person; an actual zombie who is animated by accursed culture and so its whole purpose is to kill what ever aspects of life it might see in you. What I am here saying (seeing!) has been brought to me on too many occasions – like a recurring lesson of life that I am destined to innerstand. I have seen it in too many people to the extent that I am now quite impelled by strong inner urgings and to tell the world – but would they hear it?

At the present, I am in a concrete and cast-iron cell with a perfect example of the dead who has been endowed with a sense of animation by cultural chant and mantra. This one fella, a 27-year old

"Black Male" has been successfully murdered by a certain diesis – that is, the double-edged dagger of a life sentence and of his own self-abnegation. This is no doubt, a hard way for any one to die – in civil freedom and in self-actualization. Consequently, this fella has become one of the Devil's chief advocates – a "stealth killer" that conceals itself behind a cunning network of power, force and people that he does not rightly apprehend. What I am revealing is that of extreme import – particularly for those of us who are yet alive, but who are nevertheless, in vulnerable states of naiveté and ignorance. Politically speaking, we might count this fella (my cellie) amongst those who have been "culturally kidnapped" and thus oriented (educated) to collaborate with the enemy (The Hidden Faces) and who must necessarily hate the Truth. Here now, we arrive at a grave reality: to wit all zombies are frontline soldiers; they are all expendable cogs in a relentless warfare of which they will promptly deny, and yet, will fight with wild-eyed passion, all at the same time. Imagine that. Imagine being (as you are!) engaged in crucial conflict with all kinds of clones, zombies, manikins, freaks, fiends and strange beasts of the field and yet, while you struggle and fight to stay alive (winning is based on spiritual degrees of ascent) nothing – no body will readily admit that there is (indeed!) a deadly war going on. This collective indifference and blatant denial of witchery and war is (in and of itself) the means and ways of committing *Bloodless Murder* – conscience is mocked and confidence is constantly challenged. People cease to fight and thus seek acceptance and pleasant escapades rather than the actual cause of all the wordless misery and death. When (if) you still insist on making clear and comprehensive mention of this "Mortal Combat", then you can rest assured that a zombie will be one of the first to make the attempt to undermine your voice and vision and will go even further as to convince you (if it could) to surrender and die without resistance. The Reader must innerstand that the more one defines and describes the different phases of this "Protracted Warfare", the more one will stand out as a True Light and veritable threat to the network of power, force and people – and of course, within the wake of the "Spiritual Warlord of God", the illegitimacy of the zombie is exposed. This is really what it amounts to, believe me! I know what I speak because this has been the hidden hub of the

Uncensored!

loud and acrimonious arguments that have been here and there, taking place betwixt me and this fella – my cellie. But now, if the ignorant and the auslander were to hear these verbal spats, they would readily see the deeper, more accurate interpretation of the shouts and the vicious rebukes.

The *Secret Art of Bloodless Murder* abounds in the marked deviation from moral rectitude and sound thinking – this is the first point of import because if you do not have an accurate perception of what is right and wrong, good and evil, etc. and you are not functioning with a sound mind, then there is no possible way that you could have any real regard for human rights to life. The *Secret Art of Bloodless Murder* – its indirectness and deliberate obscurity of essential Truths and Facts is the aggressive double entendre – the active pull into two opposite directions at the same time, a bright smile that conceals the burning hatred of the sublime nature, the Judas Iscariot kiss of betrayal unto death, a Trojan Horse – the elaborate gift that is given for the expressed purpose to kill from the inside. It is those who will discourage and depress you, while at the same time presenting themselves as being your must trustworthy friends. It is the studied attempt to convince you of a lie, the jealous maneuver against one's noble purposes and ambitions, the envious intrusion upon one's inner peace and comfort zones, and the undeclared war in a psychological fashion – bluffs threats, provocations, indirect disrespect, intimidations, subtle suggestions, deception, seduction, etc., all of which is designed for the purpose of creating confusion, indecision, and breakdown of self-confidence and personal strivings. *Bloodless Murder.*

Herein lies buried a world of unseen activities, Beloved Reader - if you can just see it! This war that we are all engaged in is quite mind-boggling and weird, wicked and supernatural. This is because our enemy is an aggressive opponent who is diametrically opposed to our personal (spiritual) growth and happiness – but, who faithfully speaks the language of faith and goodwill, all at the same time. This avowed enemy affronts and stabs at us from multifarious points of position and it wants nothing less than to get us out of our true selves. The arch-enemy resides in our lower nature and it expresses itself in anything and anybody it holds captive and locked in its dark domains of endless night and shadows. This nation was built on fraud, force and secret art. Thus, we must somehow wean ourselves from the poisonous pap of the wicked witch that sits upon the face of many waters. I am not advocating a violent overthrow of the United States – any revolution that is not realized first in the souls of men is a reactionary response to adverse stimulations that will not be overcome in the wake of the transformation of wealth, positions of power, or socio-economic and political institutions. What I am advocating, however, is a refined type of nihilism which is a mindset that does not lend any credence to western wizardry or the Cain-Materialists. In other words, I'm talking about a real resurrection (revolution!) of the dead – freedom from the distinguished character and the sadistic sentiments, immoral nature, misguiding beliefs and the debased value systems of "racist-capitalist-industrial-advanced technological-democracy." Again, I am not advocating reform through acts of terrorism and assassination – I'm talking about the reversal of the *Secret Art of Bloodless Murder.* In conclusion, I hasten to say that so far, as my central focus has been upon the California Prisoner, I have also attempted to include the so-called Free Citizen as well, and for as much as I have been dealing with certain points of modern penal institutions. I have also thought to extend the ideas over into the so-called Free Societies. The concept of the Zombie was born, of course out of the scandalous tricks wrought by my former cell mate– I had to eventually get away from that persistent problem. However, I am one to say that it is wise to learn from your enemies. After much wrestling, mostly within myself, I have composed something of a decent thought. Receive it, Dear Reader, ponder its possibilities – for, we have only just begun to see the inevitable rise of the True sun.

Sincerely purposeful,
O.G.

Respect

How dare the Afrikan mothers and fathers of civilization be disrespected by other so-called races? They are our children, even science has proven that. Refer to my article 'Mother of Humanity' where I explain how the world has been taught knowledge and wisdom. Most of who were poor students and incapable of grasping the higher knowledge, but now they steal credit for divine wisdom and knowledge and claim it as their own. Our thousands and even millions of years of observation and living moral and civil is discounted for their modern and minimal existence in the course of time. They have become so egotistical and arrogant that the primordial man has been strategically omitted from ancient history. They all need their asses whooped!

Science has proven that only one people have independent origin and it isn't any of them, yet they all have the audacity to claim to be native to land but I guess this is what happens when parents allow their children to run their home, and I'm talking about the planet when I say 'home'. Chaos runs freely. CraKKKers aren't the only villains to claim what existed before them. We've been on every continent as Afrikans before any colonization of us and long before forced miscegenation or better yet, rape. This information is all documented. We've been in so-called AmeriKKKa for at least 100,000 years. They will hate to hear this, but the Lemurians were very Afrikan (black). Look up the term 'Indian' and find out what it really means and where they come from. How do some of them disassociate themselves from their Afrikan parents? Mayans are descendants of Afrikans and Mayans did not educate the world as some would theorize. Many cultures have contributed, but it is without question that Afrikans were the forerunners of high science and wisdom. This is why the world came to TaMerry the beloved land also called KMT (Kemet) or the European term Egypt to learn all of the wisdom and sciences. No disrespect to the Mayans, but the Twa is considered the first lunar, stellar and solar people to map out the cosmic universe accurately. California was named after an Afrikan woman. The Folsom people were Afrikan. Pio Pico was an

Afrikan with a Spanish name hence, Pico Blvd. I guess we forgot where the Spaniards conquered. The remains of Luzia in Brazil have been proven to be Afrikan of course and compared to Dinkenesh or Lucy of Kush (Ethiopia). The Penon woman and the Pericues of Baja California and Mexico are considered Aborigine or Negrito and can easily be traced back to the Afrikan Bushmen and their culture. The Omecas of course were Afrikan.

For some reason the unspoken belief is that the Afrikans before the ancient remains in Chad, Kenya and Dinkenesh of Kush (Ethiopia) and afterwards, didn't even leave the region now called Afrika. We know this isn't rational and logical thinking. They are the only people with independent origin so where did the other people on other continents come from? This is what they teach in universities and this isn't rational. How ignorant for one to think that Afrikans never left Afrika? Let me prove it to you. Who were the Grimaldi of Europe and who are the Naga of India, the Nakhi of Japan, the Ainu of China and Japan, the Vedda of Sri Lanka, the Agta of the Philippines, the Mani of Thailand, the Ngoh of Malaysia, the Yanomani Indians of Venezuela and Brazil, the Aborigines of Australia, the massacred Tasmanians and also West Papuans? These people also exist in Iraq, Iran, Pakistan, Afghanistan, Taiwan, Yemen, Cambodia, Papua New Guinea, Cuba and Panama. Didn't Hugo Chavez tell us this? You've just finished your written trip around the world and there are many other places. These are all considered Negritos and are all descendants of the Twa or Pygmies would be the European derogatory term for these original children of the sun. My Power Point presentation on the Twa further documents these statements. These people represent the ancient or descendants of the ancient people on every continent. AFRIKAN HISTORY IS WORLD HISTORY. The great John Henrik Clarke was absolutely correct in uttering those words. Where do you think the Elamites, Sumerians, Natuffians and Akkadians came from? The people located in what you would call the Middle East didn't look that way in ancient times before modern day European invasion. They and we will respect our story simply due to the fact that without our history, theirs don't exist. We will restore ourselves having fallen from grace but we will not be disrespected in the meantime by anyone.

Uncensored!

Egyptology is a so-called modern science that only exists to debase, dehumanize and colonize the history of KMT and ancient Afrikan world history in general. We will not allow the anti-Kemetism and anti-Afrikanism that exist by our 'children'. Imagine the world without the Afrikan presence. You can't, so stop trying. We're so old no one knows how ancient we really are. We are so old, names like Kush, Alkebulan, Pangia, TaMerry, Takenset, Punt, Tanahesi, Ta-seti, Nigrecia and Afruika are fairly new names and they are considered ancient. How ignorant for one to think we never left the region called Afrika. We were here long before pole shifts and continental drifts. The world wouldn't know how to wipe their asses if it weren't for Afrikans. If they didn't know, now they know. Respect the children of the sun, the Triple O.G mother and father.

RETROSPECTIVE

Racism in the Media

I guess this piece was sparked by a mind control movie called 'Freedom Writers'. This movie is geared towards the youth. What is interesting about this movie is how the audience is once again forced to watch and feel or be sympathetic to someone else's history as oppose to their own. As usual, the Jewish Holocaust is subliminally shoved down the throats of the viewers as if Afrikans haven't had their own atrocity which no event on this planet can compare too. What is even more interesting was that there was no mention of the Afrikans that perished in the Jewish Holocaust. I guess they forgot that the Germans were involved in the slave trade as well. The Jewish-owned media has helped to perpetuate a type of Jewish arrogance and ignorance that the Holocaust is the ultimate experience of victimization and dehumanization, and that we should be more sympathetic to their history as oppose to our own as if they should be the benchmark for comparison. This is a very covert yet overt way of desensitizing folks away from Jewish desecration and total disrespect for the Afrikan culture they have cleverly stolen and bastardized. They didn't want apologies for the Holocaust. They wanted reparations and received them. Of course it's just white folk paying white folk for what they've done to each other yet the Jewish and white folk (the same people only distinguished differently by religion) have enough gull to refuse reparations to Afrikans they both dehumanized and still dehumanize. What Hypocrites!

The majority of these "problem" students were of course black so wouldn't it make sense for them to be connected to their own historical experiences. I don't recall even seeing a black teacher in the movie. Of course the teacher was white as if black teachers weren't prevalent in the public school system or in general. It was a brother on the school board, but of course he had to be persuaded by the savoir white teacher to care or take any action for students that looked like him. Once again the image of the oppressor is being shown as the savior for these remedial at-risk high school students. Wouldn't it have made more sense for the teacher to be someone who could relate to the societal problems these students dealt with as oppose to a white teacher from a rich well to do family from the suburbs that can't at all relate to these students on absolutely any level? Even more interesting was that there was never a discussion that really dealt with the aspect of Global White Supremacy and how that dictates the curriculum and has a lot to do with society's issues these students deal with. Were there not any Afrikan books these students could read or any films these students could watch in regards to their history? Were there not museums they could've been exposed to? Naturally they would go to the holocaust museum and read the book of a holocaust survivor, now wouldn't they? In the end she would become their decorated hero instead of their own mothers and fathers, or a hero in their own image. What about the countless slaves that revolted against a wicked system of slave masters and oppression and our ancient history eons before that and Europeans? Once again it is purposely implemented in a movie that Afrikans have no history worth talking about. I recognized in the first 15 minutes of this movie this was psychological warfare hidden behind a story about art and triumph that once again showed the so-called Jews as victims and heroes strategically in the same format. The media is so saturated with this that not many recognize their involvement in Afrikan dehumanization historically and present. They only show Afrikans in the news as criminals. The majority of roles given to blacks in Hollywood are crack heads, broken families, rappers, athletes and prostitutes. I won't even mention Jewish owned B.E.T. The movie Hollywood Shuffle is some real ass shit. This is why they dare not show your story through their media outlets. You would recognize that Hitler was only the instrument karma used to manifest the law of attraction and if I forgot to mention, the so-called Jews do own the majority of major media outlets. The so-called Jews don't want us to know about their names on the slave ships, ownership of the slave ships and their money that funded and still fund slavery, capitalism and imperialism. The Jewish and this government have done things to make Hitler look like a petty criminal. That is the truth whether you like it or not! They took part in our atrocity and capitalized from it. I'm pretty certain that we had absolutely nothing to do with what the Germans did to them. We were also victims. Would that be outright racism and discrimination that Afrikans aren't mentioned? It's not an accident! Who is really being victimized in the media?

Uncensored!

Hip-Hop Part 1
'What's Hot'

by Derek Chase

Controlling the content of what you listen to on a daily basis is a huge step in the deprogramming process. Hip-Hop is one of the main tools euro-peons use to program the youth in the Afrikan community towards self-destruction. If you observe the transformation Hip-Hop has taken since its inception, you can easily see the effect it has had in determining the values of Afrikan youth. From Red, Black and Green Afrika medallions, to chains with spinning tire pendants, the influence is obvious. If Lil Jon was screaming about strengthening the black community, educating our own children and forcing the pigs out of our neighborhoods instead of "skeetin'" and "shakin' it like a salt shaker", the values of the youth would be drastically different. Hip-Hop music had been manipulated and transformed from promoting black unity, revolution and individuality, into some house nigga, minstrel show, blackface bullshit that degrades our Queens, promotes consumption and material worship and got young Neters in the hood dressing exactly alike. These kids are walking around looking like the black version of the Backstreet Boys. If I see another group of ten young men all dressed up in white T's, blue jeans and white tennis shoes, I'm gonna run up and slap the shit out of them dudes myself. You got a generation of young black men out of shape like a bunch of cracka's 'cause they don't wanna play sports any more. They'd rather put on white t-shirts and stand around in a group listening to Mike Jones and Dipset ringtones on the latest Boost Mobile phones that they convinced their dumb ass parents to buy. Yes, that's right, I called their parents dumb. Dumb as fuck for letting their children listen to The Beat, Power 106 or any of these corporate-controlled, poison-producing radio stations. Dumb as shit for letting their kids watch BET, MTV, VH-1 or any of these other faggot ass video stations that show half-naked and confused Afrikan Goddesses being exploited and objectified by lost Afrikan Gods with platinum in their teeth. Yes, these parents are stupid as a mother fucker who

93

Uncensored!

believes that Jesus was white, or somebody who believes that the Towers were blown up by someone other than the United Snakes Government in order to advocate a war with more people of Afrikan descent that we now think we are better than. I promise you, if my children come in the house singin' any of that bullshit, I'm gonna beat they ass like they married a cracka. But yet I do digress. Any person without a blindfold on and earplugs in their ears can list hundreds of rap artists who suck, like 50 Cent, Nelly and Ying Yang Twinz. What most people don't know, because of these honkey's trying to keep the knowledge suppressed, is that the list of dope emcees, although a little harder to uncover, is just as long. As Hip-Hop connoisseurs, Imhotep (*Hip-Hop Part 2*) and I have taken it upon ourselves to compile a list of some of the emcees whitey don't want you to know about. For those of you looking for an alternative to the garbage the Young Jeezy's and D4L's provides us with, here is a short list to get you started.

E Rule	Wordsworth	Living Legends Immortal
Technique	Common	Planet Asia
Dead Prez	P.O.W.	Supernatural
Self Scientific	Hawk and Rip/NYM	Nas
Paris	Ise Lyfe	K-OS
Hassan Salam	Ras Kass	Crooked I
Talib Kweli	Jean Grae	F.T.P.
Mos Def	Murs	Pharoahe Monch
Saigon	KRS 1	Rakim
Juice	Royce Da 5'9"	Chino XL
The Roots	Gangstarr	Dialated Peoples

It's time that we expose these coons, hold them accountable and replace them with the real. These house niggas are doing the cracka's work for them and poisoning our babies. To quote one of the illest emcees in the game, Talib Kweli, "We're poisoning our seeds before they can grow. If you poison my seed, you've got to go."

Hip-Hop Part 2
'What's Not Hot'
by Imhotep Musa-Cushan

What's not hot in Hip-Hop is the bamboozled coons running around talking about nothing… "Grills…Ice…Sex" on some straight Sambo shit. Always showing their teeth or as they say, "their grill" (iced out of course), not knowing that they are part of a monopoly – culture exploitation at its highest level when you overstand the importance of music to us as a people. The most prevalent thing in Hip-Hop is the beat, in retrospect to the drums. Although many of us have assimilated into this society and lost our roots, it can't be denied that drums move us! Afrikan drums connect to our spirit (KA) and our soul (BA)…we need drums! In Afrikan dance groups, the dancer (or listener in our case) feed off the energy of the drum. The sound (frequencies) of the drum get into our being until our body is controlled by it. Due to the effects of the drums, this is why one may find oneself bumping their heads to some of the nonsense called music that is plaguing Hip-Hop.

Drums, especially in R.A.P. (Rhythmic Afrikan Poetry), can cause many different emotions and feelings. Not to mention the drum creates spiritual connections to Deities, Ancestors and Orishas. As a matter of fact, drums were so powerful that crackers forbade our ancestors from playing them on plantations because of the energy they channeled or conjured. So in today's time, these crackers overstand that they don't have to take away the beat of the drum away from us. All they have to do is control the beat and use it against us. Basically, they've realized that a change in societal conditions called for a change in oppressive tactics (hint-hint: that means guise more modern technologically advanced plantation methodologies). This is what's going on today in Hip-Hop! They have saturated Hip-Hop with ignorant, slave assed, bamboozled coons who do nothing but channel negative energy over the drum's true intent, in turn killing the healing effect of the drum. They have also managed to change the frequency of the instruments to such a

Uncensored!

degree that it no longer agrees with the genetic make-up of us as a people.

No longer do you hear messages like P.E., X-Clan, Dead Prez, P.O.W., etc. on the airwaves. Instead you are spoon-fed slave assed, bamboozled, coon artists like D4L 'Laffy Taffy', Juelz Santana 'Here We Go - The Whistle Song', Dem Franchise Boys 'Boy I Think They Like Me', Mike Jones and a host of southern plantation slave assed rappers! Like I said, different era but the same old tactics are yielding crackers' desired effects... continued enslavement and ignorance of the original people!

Terrorists of the Arts

El Hajj Malik Shabazz (Malcolm X) said it best, "We must recapture our heritage and our identity if we are ever to liberate ourselves from the bonds of white supremacy. We must launch a cultural revolution to un-brainwash an entire people." We know that the government and some artists themselves desecrate the manifestation of creativity. He or she who exploits the arts is the enemy. Art was never seen as or used as solely entertainment until Euro "peons" colonized and co-opted the spiritual and creative essence of it. The music industry and hip-hop are prime examples of this. According to the ancient Afrikans (the creators of art), the artist is supposed to be a conduit between the spiritual realm and the physical/material realm. Now its role has been redefined and diminished by its Euro "peon" sponsors of present who I refer to as "ARTISTIC TERRORISTS". The exploitation and minstrelism devalues and demoralizes the importance of it politically, socially and culturally. Amiri Baraka clearly states, "The danger is its co-optation by imperialism so eureka we get a host of Kenny G. poets".

In the McCarthy era any artist that had an anti-government sentiment, spoke of liberation as well as spoke truth to power was labeled as a communist and heavily maligned by the fascist system. Doesn't communist sound like terrorist? Some artists bitched out. Many of whom you honor today while others stood by their work and morals and continued to bang on the system despite the repercussions.

Art is every aspect of revolution when in its highest form. Its energy historically has the capability and capacity to transcend and ascend beyond circumstance. The oppressive states program is to suppress the role of the artist which is to be timeless, to be spiritual enlightenment for the masses, the vanguard for critical and analytical thought that moves the people, to bring clarity to humanity when inhumane, to create what has yet to be created, to be brutally honest, to instill vision, hindsight, insight, and wisdom, to give solutions and to not give a fuck about political correctness, the status quo or conformity. The artist must tap into their spirit and soul

Uncensored!

to be a vessel for the ancestors to speak through the art form and the artist must take sides. The state of global white supremacy overstands that art is energy, sound waves, vibrations and calls to action that creates or changes reality positively or negatively. <u>ART IS TO EXPOSE DESCRIPTIVELY AND SPECIFICALLY THE GRISLY, SAVAGE AND MORBID INSIDES OF THIS GESTAPO GOVERNMENT OF IMPERIALISM, FASCISM AND CLASSISM</u>. The artist must create and be the reality that dismantles immorality, corruptness, barbarism, backwardness and de-evolution .We must show vivid and graphic pictures and images through ALL aspects of art. Exert intuition and honest expression. Why mimic those who mimic us? Or those who exploit and capitalize the lower nature of the art form they impose? We must be a weapon against oppression. Be a sniper with words. Be a suicide bomber with the paint brush. Be a strategist in song. This is when the cowboy government chooses to contradict the so-called 1st amendment right of freedom of speech when used against their hypocritical asses. This is why they classify some artists as terrorists. We must not be the masses of manipulated sheep exploited by AmeriKKKan <u>ARTISTIC TERRORISM</u> which cuts out tongues literally and control the thoughts of the people with spiritual, psychological and sometimes even physical warfare.

Mother of Humanity

Patriarchy, misogyny and feminism has constructed a strategic assault on the Goddess state and energy that sustains the universe's life force. Sistas, you are the physical manifestation of the cosmic universe. Your womb is the gateway of the all-in-one energy that continues existence of life. A walking heaven-on-earth when not imposed upon by foreign culture, beliefs and Nordic lifestyle. Your womb represents the most ancient wisdom. The first sacred humble abode existed within you. Your womb was man's first dwelling place. Now your womb has been tampered with and soiled by rotten seeds. There has also been a systematic attack on your birth canal to hinder or sterilize your ability to give birth. The spirit and soul of the Goddess concept has become de-valued, desensitized and dehumanized and now recreated into video vixens, physical objects and visions of self-hate which is lower nature.

We as Afrikan men have allowed the oppressive states' chauvinistic ego and hatred of Afrikan women to enslave us physically, psychologically and spiritually. How can our beautiful sistas not see saviors and the Creatress/Creator in her own image and likeness? Sistas, it was your energy that manifested into creation the concept of nurturing. This is most definitely not the creation or manifestation of masculine energy. Only a patriarchal society and hatred of the woman impose the degradation and dehumanization of earth's mother and cultivator who is cosmic when in her higher state of being. The closer one is to nature the closer one is to their true essence. Your menstrual cycle represents the 28 day cycle of the moon which is also linked to fertility. The spiral of your hair is in sequence with the direct spiral of the universe and operates as an antenna which links you to spiritual phenomena. No wonder the media pushes images of straight hair in your subconscious. This is a covert warfare to disconnect you.

The illusion of feminism and equality has thwarted your and our spiritual transformation and ascendance. You could never be equal to a man nor can a man be equal to you. Your cosmic role and energy is that of a woman and a man's role is that of a man. When

Uncensored!

trying to emulate masculinity you are denying yourself of your true feminine essence which causes an imbalance in relationships and dialectical law of opposites, not to mention your energy's vibration and connection to the macro universe as a whole. The rise in homosexuality is an example of that. It's time to take Greece and AmeriKKKas' perverted acts out of the bedroom and bring God, Goddess and cosmic energy back into the bedroom. Sistas, if this is something you don't overstand, then you have yet to truly experience a real orgasm. A *spiritual* orgasm is what I'm referring to.

Cosmic law will always supersede man's law. It was you that taught the world how to write and speak, and now we allow our students to dictate our history, present and future existence. It was you that birthed and developed high civilization and humanity. It is your feminine warrior spirit that still resides in your DNA code and genetic memory bank. It is man's pathological behavior and obsession with neo-colonialism, greed and control that has circumvented the uplifting of the Black Afrikan woman and women in general. As well as the illusion of a feminist movement used to further hinder the woman's role in the universe, not AmeriKKKa, but the universe. Why assert yourself as men when there are already men to do that? The feminist movement only is and was patriarchy masked and disguised in white feminism which exploited sistas while elevating white women and homosexuality. The female principle is demeaned in a patriarchal paradigm. Our people historically was matrilineal and matriarchal paying homage and praise to the woman before being Europeanized and mis-educated to look outward instead of inward towards your own innate power, spirit and energy force that resonates beyond the physical. Anti-female religious doctrine doesn't aid in the spiritual development and re-transformation either. I say re' because you have already been there. It's time to elevate beyond the emotional state of conditioned subconscious self-hate and ignorance of one's self. Sistas, you taught white woman and every other woman how to function as women from hygiene to culture, to language, to love, etc. Your nipples breastfed humanity and now we've allowed white men and women to socially rear and dictate to you what a woman is, her roles, reality, child nurturing, state of being and how to operate in your relationships and family. Brothas, we must embrace our sistas and procreate with our sistas the images of our mothers and fathers and our fore-parents. We must procreate the black messiahs, male and female. What was once sacred has now been desecrated by people who try to imitate and mimic you, but they can't mimic nature's mother and the all-in-one energy that resides within you. They can only attempt to destroy you which in turn will destroy them. You are the antithesis and genesis of every culture's story. When the Afrikan woman is desecrated, all of humanity is desecrated. There is NO revolution without you. The doorway to our freedom is still open and the ancients still echo "<u>KNOW THYSELF</u>!"

"The original family is the universal solution
If real fathers stepped up as fathers
If real mothers stepped up as mothers
If sisters and brothers bonded together
To help rebuild the family structure that was stolen
Then once again our legacy will be golden!"

Lorenzo

The Word!

Cave Ho

This white girl and caveman
Tried to impose themselves on me
These sick, evil
Disease infested
Blue eyed, blond hair
Ain't got no ass
No spirit
Cavewoman
Ice Age ho, trailer trash, trailer park
White boy lack melanin
Wanna be
Jew
Stole our Heru Lock
Original crack pipe queen
Hairy back, knuckle crawler
Maggot attracter
Trying to impose themselves on me
My Dinkenesh sistas tried to civilize them
Now she tries to imitate her
She wants my tree inside her
She wants to know what it's like to manifest God
She tired of fighting melanoma
Fake ass skin tan
Collagen lip injected
Breast and ass implant infected
Caveman takes pills for penis girth
Who got the natural big and potent one
They got a war against our seed
We sustain the earth
They desecrate the earth
Cave bitch know I descend from the Twa
Still eat their meat bloody, uncooked and raw
She be animalistic, barbaric, cannibalistic
Cleopatra
Fake ass queen
Wanna be
Wish she was Sobek Neferu

Flaming white boy wished it too
Even perverted Romans tried to emulate Queen T
Even the rain couldn't clean their mange and filth
Under armpit smellin' like musk ass
Diseased and polluted every land they went to
Polluted the drinking water
Pissed and shitted in the Nile
Biological and chemical warfare
Genocide
Theft, wretchedness
Everywhere they stepped foot on this planet
4,000 years of anti-nature, anti-life
Homosexuality
No connection with the universe
You and your Cro-Magnum man are not hue-man
You are the existence of theories
All debatable
My sistas are the fulfillment of existence
True reality, un-debatable
The black woman that birthed me
Fulfillment of all prophecy
White woman thought menstrual cycle was unearthly
You will never deserve me
The father of humanity
You are depopulating
Black women had to nurse your children
We take back the seed of Tehuti
Now micro and macro womb can have a spiritual baby
Once brothas and sistas stop fucking with
These sick, evil
Disease infested
Blue eyed, blond haired
Ain't got no ass
No lips
No hips
No rhythm
No soul
No concept of nature
Cavewoman
Ice Age ho
White boy lackin' melanin

Wanna be
Jew
Fake Holy Land
Stole our Heru Lock
Original crack pipe queen, hairy back, knuckle crawler
Maggot attracter
Trailer park, trailer trash
Calcified pineal gland
Trying to impose their inhumane selves on me
And that's that piece!

Uncensored!

Dictatorship

Do Kenyans receive aid
If they refuse to accept Jesus
4.5 million enslaved by water deprivation n Kenya
Food deprivation
Medical deprivation
Pimped for resources
Resources pimped by anti-nature pimp
Sudan is demobilized by mobilized slave hand
President Aristeed kidnapped from Haiti
U.S Co-Ops Cops cover up new age cointelpro
Ask Cynthia
U.S never forgot Haitian revolution
Nor did France and Britain
Patrice Lumumba ousted from Congo by paramilitary militia
Anglos got 22nd century surveillance on afros
U.S might wanna think twice before fuckin' wit Castro
Cause Cuba ain't divided
Cuba ain't forgot Cuban missile crisis
Just as AmeriKKKa ain't forgot anthrax threat
What happened to it?
Paranoia
Bush can't duplicate Kush
He too savage
Rainbow Coalition still pushin' PUSH
N.A.A.C.P still answers to a Jew
U.N.C.F too
How does neo new global world war order affect u?
All part of J. Edgar Hoover's cloned Klan's plan
Ain't no split between north and south
Just white conservatives
Liberals just as racial
Soon as I mention homosexuality and reparation
Mention how they benefit
From the labor on the plantation

Uncensored!

Missionaries imposing Christianity
Tryin' 2 aid Afrikans
With the same thing that enslaved us
Euro "peons" tryin' to suppress their guilt with philanthropy
Doesn't change economic disparity
So-called inequality
Human or civil
Police terrorism
Like officer Hatfield on STANLEY MILLER
Jeremy Morse on DONOVAN JACKSON
Edward Larrigan on MARGARET MITCHELL
4 Riverside policemen on TYISHA MILLER
4 L.A.P.D policemen on RODNEY KING
Name, names
No change n ghetto concentration camps
No change n political poverty pimps
No change n political platforms
That continues to form white supremacy covertly
Ask puppet Indonesian government for U.S
Who depopulate
Massacre
Dehumanize
Provoke genocide on West Papuans
Like Australians on Aborigines
Decapitated Tasmanians
White slave hand backslap the Sudan
While white Egyptology invents Afrikan history
Uncle Sam be a product of secret society incest
Protest be flog marks to U.S Republic
Movement became generic
While barbaric conquerors plant flags n Baghdad
Deprive unarmed civilians of humanity
Drop bioengineered food 2 children
Rape virgins
Food laced with biochemical warfare
Thousands of Iraqis killed
They used to be Sumerians
Migrated Afrikans

Raped by euro "peon" foreign invasions
Long before Arabs
Impossible 2 estimate number of Afrikans in the Diasporas
Who perished due to barbaric nature of a blond man
No time 2 surrender
Power structure declares war in this new age
DICTATORSHIP

Uncensored!

U

U said it's the warrior in my voice that u crave
Yo' life force pimp slaps eternity
U tongue tie messiahs
U chastise prophets
When her hips sway from side 2 side
She humbles gravity
I like the Red, Black and Green in her switch
The arch n her mid back puts inertia at a standstill
I love the fact that
I can't run my fingers through her hair
Her mannerism mime
Rhyme couldn't depict her wise skin
U speak n jimbay motha tongue
Warrior Goddess protecting her micro womb
Soul songs croon n yo' sacred abode

U grant liberation,, when u suck my bottom lip
Ain't no hypocrisy n yo' hips
I lay Black Power n the smile of yo' dimple
I'm the crease n yo' bellbottom
I wanna lick yo' soul wit my spirit
Don't call me daddy cause that sounds like incest
The ancestors adore u
U r the epitome of infinity
Time envies u like jealousy
Infinity echoes u like plagiarized scripture
I lay shea butter on blistered arch of feet
Yo' uterus disciplines time
U r timeless like attribute
I wanna impregnate yo' spirit,,
So we can procreate karma
I make love 2 yo' wombs aura
Tickle yo' lower chakra
U manifest the astral projected chi n me
U said love is revolution and revolution is love

111
Uncensored!

U dictate the celestial moon phase every month
U fruition the elements
No mo cotton fields bruising yo' footprints
Eternity mimics the thought of u
Yo' soul transforms like meticulous metamorphosis
If heaven existed it would be the scent of u
Somewhere between yo' locks or afro is the deified dimension
I know yo' soul is still swollen from fighting for freedom

U make beauty content
That moment between every heartbeat
Is me paying homage 2 u
The true rhythm of yo' wisdom is antiquity
I like how u tilt yo' b-bop from side 2 side
U fly like fly-away collas and Angela Davis' old afro
U r womb of afrocentric soul
I love when u say free' em all and all power to the people
U r art not yet 2 be personified
U r sweet back taste so lovely
Sweet honey thigh
I wanna make love 2 the scent between yo' thighs
I love the Red, Black and Green n yo' switch
U consume the all n one energy
U

Uncensored!

Genocide

How can generation after generation
Repeat itself for the worst
How can we stop the GENOCIDE
That happens within families
This God awful curse
The madness that our young black men feel
Within not knowing where to begin in life
This, their fathers did not teach them
Their mothers could not reach them
Brought up by two hands instead of four
Watching dad walk out the door or was there another man
that their mother slept with before,
which ever one it was, neither one was there
Why should we expect them to care?
I am my mother's child which she had to bare
Who said life was fair?
Our little girls gone wild
Having to bare a child at the age of fifteen
Who said this world was mean
I mean, we all knew
This young black girl was going to be a statistic
Living in a world that's gone ballistic
Music blasting the sounds of words that's unrealistic
Don't mention the devil's playground
Television pushing our children to make the wrong decision
Rapper's words are bond
Parent's words are gone
In one ear and out the other
Growing up by the hands of an unsophisticated brother
We need to pull together
Black sisters and brothers
Stick together and take care of one another
Educate the young ones
Even if they don't belong to you

Uncensored!

If there are only a few that we can get through
It still makes a difference because they are the key to our future
and the solution to the pollution in the black soul
that's growing cold among us
It's like a fungus spreading
Against our black population
Stop the GENOCIDE
The deliberate and systematic destruction of
A racial
Political
Or cultural group
Stop the GENOCIDE
It's happening right here
And you don't have to look worldwide

Written by
Racshel

Extrasensory

U gotta be a spirit
U gotta be a soul
U gotta be energy
U gotta be transformation
Exist n meditation
Maximize the minimal
Slap mediocrity n the face
U be the original monk
Be God and Goddess
Live off the air
The land
Nature
Intuition
Become one with yo' chambers
Be able to tap into alchemy
Create existence with the 96% of yo' brain
that lies dormant so 4% couldn't be intelligent
Know what sounds elevate 1st and 2nd chambers
3rd and 4th chambers to lungs
5th chamber physically and orally
6th chamber to procreation
7th chamber to so-called immune system
U gotta win the war within yo' own trinity
Step to Orion
The God exists inside God
Not outside of God
Transform from plane to plane
Dimension 2 dimension
U only see what u allow yourself 2 c
Take limitations off of self
U gotta see what u afraid 2 c
Stop being a punk
Walk with yo' left foot forward
Close yo' eyes and open yo' mind

Uncensored!

The only thing that exist is what u allow 2 exist
Not knowing self gives power 2 the powerless
Be the embodiment of Ra
Be Ptah
Be Tehuti
All that is u
So be u
Cause that is u
Auset too
Manifest Per Em Heru
Take back yo' square
Be instincts
Tongue be words
Words be tongue
Tongue be sound
Be all of that
Exist even outside of that
Sound be vibrational complex element
Be complex yet simple
Massage your temple
Vibrate like elements
Insert spirit into frequency
Make sonar field
Feel
Positive energy
Be contrary to illness and dis-ease
Spirit never dies
It transforms
No material price on it
Spiritual over material
Moral over immoral
Transformation of spirit supersedes physical
Beyond yo' five material senses
Somewhere within and beyond the 4 senses
U have yet 2 adventure
Move like the spirit

Uncensored!

Guilty

We declare this government guilty
Guilty of police terrorism on
AMADOU DIALO
ROY ZEAL
ABNER LOUIMA
ANTHONY BAEZ
LATASHA MILLER
MARGARET MITCHELL
DEONDRE BRUNSTON
KEISHIA BRUNSTON
92-YEAR OLD KATHRYN JOHNSTON
DONOVAN JACKSON
DEVON BROWN
MARTIN LEE ANDERSON
SEAN BELL
WILLIE RICKS MUKASA DADA
FRANK JUDE
GUSTAVO RUGLY
19-MONTH OLD SUSIE PENA

GUILTY
Guilty of barbarism
Savagery
PERVERSION
Gentrification
Painting the Yashua white, and renaming him Jesus
Distorting God concept
CLAIMING TO BE THE REAL JEWS
Counterfeit religion
Lack of spirituality
Bondage
Feminism
Images of a white Tutankhamen
A white Nefertiti

White Madonnas and White Marys
Lying about the ancient people of KMT having slaves
Aliens building the pyramids
GUILTY
Of war crime convictions
Imposing sanctions
The Korean War
Hiroshima
9-11
Settler colonies
Trying 2 colonize time
Embezzlement
MONEY LAUNDERING
Patriarchy
Commercialism
Changing Goddess to God
The misinterpretation of Heaven and Hell
Sterilization
Calcification of melanin

GUILTY
Of stock market crashes
Peonage
Unemployment
Underemployment
Exploitation of hip hop the new auction block
Promoting minstrelism
ZIONIST PROTOCOLS
Cultism
Class war
FASCISM
Burnings at the stake
GLOBAL WHITE SUPREMACY
Impunity
Impurity
Insanity
IMMORALITY
Sharpsville Massacre

Uncensored!

Tulsa, Oklahoma
Rosewood
Greensville
The ritualistic character of lynching that still exist
N gas chambers
Lethal injections

GUILTY
OF POLITICAL ASSASSINATIONS
THE CRIMINALIZATION of
POLITICAL PRISONERS
U know who they are so call out their names
GUILTY
Of air strikes n Pakistan
No 40 acres and a mule
Theft and plagiarism of high civilization
Feminization
Wire tapping scandals
HOMOSEXUALITY
SODOMY
Misogyny
PEDOPHILIA
COUP D' ÉTATS
GUILTY
Of demonic religious rituals
Idol Gods
False images
Biochips
Bioengineered food
FALSE PROPHETS
Disdain
HIDING TRUTH
Co-optation
THIS GOVERNMENT IS GUILTY OF
LYING ABOUT ITS TRUE IDENTITY
AIDS
SYPHILLIS
EBOLA

Uncensored!

TUSKEGEE
Contamination of the universe
Neo-right wing conservatism
FRAUD EGYPTOLOGY
FRAUD EDUCATION
Poverty
Mass manipulation
Stolen land
Alien concepts
Psychological warfare
Spiritual warfare
INHUMANITY
Sweatshops
GUILTY
Of Tsunamis
The Depression
Occupation
Stolen resources
Psychopathic elitism
Ghettos
Dogma
Gang injunctions
Infiltration
Flooding the streets with crack
Ethnic cleansing
The disguise of assimilation
Acculturation
Subliminal mind control
White collar crime
Blue collar crime
Stealing Wall Street
Weapons of mass destruction
The bombing of Libya
Somalia
Sudan
Iraq
Afghanistan
The levees n New Orleans

Uncensored!

Guilty
Of raping Prisoners of War
Guilty
Of terrorist cells
The House
Senate
Congress
C.I.A
F.B.I
Are all GUILTY
Of not acknowledging any of these things
WE THE PEOPLE DECLARE THIS GOVERNMENT GUILTY
And the sentence is
CALAMITY
GUILTY!!!!!!!!!
GUILTY!!!!!!!!!!!
GUILTY!!!!!!!!!!!!!

*"When the oppressor defines freedom
He continues to re-invent slavery"*

Sadiki Bakari

Bum

Ghetto inhabitant
Species of
Fake 14k gold
Platinum wanna be
Wallabe
Knick kickas
Played out
Don't come back
Came back
Dirty cargo slack wearin' blunt junky bum
B-bop to hip hop
Boom box jammin'
Diploma on momma's wall
No education
Conk hair style wearin' mothafucka
Funky breath
Nipple rings and hair grease combed out
Smellin' up the spot like drunk under armpit musk
Perry Ellis hustling
Millionaire turned dope pusher
Basket pusher
Black lip from finger tip resin
Grown man searchin'
Cracked out wit county check n hand
Indictments
Child support callin'
Ambitious
Food stamp collector
Vegetarian
Swine eater
Used to be a writer
A project poet wit a pimps tongue
Hustled religion
Listens to acid jazz

Uncensored!

Hip-Hop exploiter
Churches Chicken
Trash can eatin'
X-con
X-rated
NBA shoe wearin' like Converse
Niggaz buy anything
Jim Dandy Chicken
No stocks/no bonds
Back of the bus chillin'
Cigarette smokin'
Nappy beard on bootie chin
On the way to Leimert Park
Wears X-hats for Black History Month
Sportin' knotted hair and tatts
Liquor bum
Hoodie pullovers
One time computer hacker
Talkin' bout
What that hit fo
7-11
You thought he crapped out
Tie wearin'
Bum cleaned himself up
No mo dime sacks
Smoked out, crack didn't kill
Media's stereotypes had you thinking he was black
He was white
Bum cleaned himself up
Hired by corporate amerikkka on sight
While we r addicted to their stereotypes

Uncensored!

Poetry

My words ain't pikkin' nat cotton
No cotton mouth over here
No mo fairytales
Pin the fairytales on the honkey
Gimmie back my tongue
We speak afrikan ebonic slang called English
A bastardized language from the British
We went from locks to shakin' dreds
Oakland went from Black Power Movements to Hyphy Movements
A new definition of ignorance
From divinity to poppin' ecstasy
From scrolls to mind control
From revolution to prostitution
Artists became hoes to their own product
Tongue use to resonate wisdom
Enslaved by their own words
Shackles on ney tongue
Pissin' on paper
Shittin' on pens
Now too many poets wanna be rappers
I could speak metaphysically
But hip-hop wouldn't understand me
Neither would spoken word
Unless I said nigga
The euro "peon" definition
The revolution won't be in a 3 minute and 10 second poem
I wish I could Velcro some poet's lips
Enslave their ego trips
But that would be censorship and the God in me
Won't let me contradict what I'm against so I stand alone
Risen like Lazarus before Lazarus
The third eye and soul that already existed in Kemet
The tongue is AFRIKAN antiquity
So why is yours straight instead of nappy?

I understand divine balance so you have to exist
Allow the oppressor to define you
How can you sell the rights to your own words?
Negro Wordsmiths
Pikkkin'
Corporate
Cotton
Once political poets
Now prophets for profit
No longer writing for the people
U write to serve your own ego
The weapon of your voice is now silenced
Political prisoner n your own mind
Went from Afrikan to Euro "peon"
From spiritual to material
They simply mimic u
And now u mimic them
A bastard child of a bastard child
And don't dare say I'm judging u
Although we know u like to be judged
No disrespect
I just lost respect for u
I would never put my son in your poetry workshop
That's like B.E.T showing real hip hop
We summon the ancestors to bring u back again
We will still be here for u
When u become a true artist again
When this part of your journey ends
POETRY

"I don't participate in slam
Because I write for a people
That can't afford to lose again."

Nikki Skies

Untitled

Uncle Sam
Not my uncle
Lo-jacked my boogie
Compromised my soul
Got on tight slacks
Slick
Slick can't breathe
Bellbottoms sway n the wind
Nappy use to dance inside rhythm
Now he's fraternal twin wit white ideology
Due to a bootleg divided culture and ghetto concentration camps
Programmed brothas' lack attention span to understand
New government swastikas and old funk era afros
Give me back my pick
Political pimps, pimp
Ankh generations
The crosses misinterpretation
Dying
Slowly
Irregularity of freedom
Never coming monthly
Slave periods never end
Just commas
New house niggaz n Asian made kente
Paralysis of mind, soul and neck
Third eye anorexia
Conditioned crying Buddha, or whoever
Clear reflections of angel dust illusions
Ill dusted angels n mirrored reflection
Refract life
Retract life
Add racism to broken down fractions isolated
I still soar despite westernization
I bare the weight of nappy lynched souls

Uncensored!

We bare the undetermined weight of mastas noose
Despite conformity
I am vibrating into the sun
Oppression dims our stairway of glow
My generation's status is soar
Next generation's rich is still poor
Our status quo have become quotes of quotas
What is status and who determines it
Quotas are by no means equality, nor reparations
The concept of equality doesn't exist anyway
They can keep their 40 acres and a mule
40 Ounces too
Shit, we fly wit no wings
We float on naps of melanin
While bliss wit ignorance

Spirit

Creator's original children
Bottled slave notes reappear
Ancient footprint n another life
Red, Black and Green turned rainbow
Desecrating the Land of the Bow
Imposed gay shit on na downbeat
Downtrodden
Caught corruptive lifestyle and try 2 justify it
Superimposed chips n brain scan
Smited the pink skin cave ho
Goddess tread n invisible flesh
Stop praying 2 Jesus
Mind control believe, belief
Now ancient motif got thin nose and straight hair
Chicken scratch on scrolls once sacred
History illusion believe n the superimposed
Heru is now side show
Hidden blackness n the greatness
Somehow foreign idolatries became main event
Conditioned consciousness works n shifts
Computer programs can't control the spirit or can they?
Religion revolts against the occult
Spirit sense 9 senses
Time ticks timid
Ask Horam Akhet
Pharaoh's spiritual doorway that inhuman man can't C
A crisis for these white-minded Negroes
Still can't get past the double consciousness
Aquarius brings the next spiritual level
We 2,000 years behind the 2,160 year cycle
Moon phase is just a phase
The sun is always shining
The imbalanced will no longer be imbalanced
Spiritual solstice is reflection of inner morals

What's immoral will no longer be yo' calcified Deity
So it has been and so will it be
Only we can realign true hue-manity
So throw away yo' so-called holy book and
Pick up nature
Realign yourself with the truth
Cause the Creator ain't wrote nothing n Greek
English
Arabic or Aramaic
Man did
Nickel and dime type niggaz
Search for exterior instead of interior
Outer instead of inner
Man's paradigm
Instead of spirits infinity
I shall bathe in the macro
While you pray to filth

Uncensored!

"Religion is man's fear of being spiritual!"

Sadiki Bakari

Uncensored!

Echoes That Cry

AmeriKKKa persecutes me
Ask me 2 salute the racist flag
Salute stars that enslaves oppression
Oppression enslaves slaves
Represent stripes that mark whelps on slave labored backs
Black backs that weep whelps
Whelps weep
Soil blistered my ancestor's feet
Feet that slept for years
They still sleep
Now soil keeps whispers that sleep
Sleep that dreams/and cry freedom
Freedom cries dreams that never wake
They sleep walk in the day
While rocking nightmares 2 sleep
Only 2 walk and whisper on soil that plant my echoes that cry
Echoes that soil my soul and hide and implant a blistered tomorrow
That whispers blisters
Tomorrow's whispers
Mark another day of Negro spirituals
Go tell it on the Mountain
Swing Lo
Wait n the Water
I ain't pickin' nat cotton no'mo
Niggaz still pickin' nat cotton
The ship sank slowly
The ship is still sinking
Anotha day of hip-hop gospels
A day of misrepresentation that we represent
Anotha day of
Pimp walkin' and crip walkin'
Slave talkin'
Jive talkin'
Smooth talkin'

Zig-zaggin' and saggin'
Shaw rollin'
High rollin'
Blunt rollin'
Blunt smokin'
Blue and red raggin'
Wall taggin'
Pistol packin'
Car jackin'
Money stackin'
Wanna be mackin'
Brothas n the back and
Getting 2 the top of corporate ameriKKKa and
Sellin' out and
Forgettin' u a black man
All part of ameriKKKas plan
Anotha day of fear
Anotha day of
I am not a slave
We are fuckin' slaves
Anotha day of distorted black families
Baby mommas and baby daddies
Anotha day of bullshit rituals and beliefs
Anotha day of getting on yo' knees and praying
Anotha day of distorted spirituality called religion
Anotha day of worshiping a white Jesus
How come the image doesn't look like you?
How can you worship yo' oppressor?
Anotha day of
Not having enough vision to see past tomorrow
Anotha day of
Separating self from Goddess and God
Anotha day of compromising
Anotha day of more bogus incarceration
Less education
Another day of poverty
Elitism
The Class system

Uncensored!

Anotha day of living someone else's reality
Another fuckin' day of
Bullshit

Fucking Wit My Mind

Somebody keeps fuckin' wit my mind
This shits become mainstream
This shits become a part of life
Changed the color of our Mandingo deities
Stole our ancient philosophy
Called it Greek
Oppressed our spirituality
Sold it back 2 us in the form of Christianity
Judaism
Islam
Catholicism
Charged us 2 buy into the reality that we r free
Putting our faith in a holy book
That's been rewritten by crooks
Stole our perception
Enslaved and co-opted symbols
Stole our sanctity
Serenity
Piece of mind
Our minds
Stealing our melanin
Culture
Closed our eyelids so we can't see
Our existence breathe like test tube babies
And what about our history?
Desecrated our civilizations
Middle passage had tragic traffic
Stolen niggaz tryin' 2 profit
Stole our sense of self
Love of self and one another
So who r we?
What were we?
What will we be?
As if I'm a mere figment of my pigment

Caucasians r playing craps with our naps
What that hit fo?
They've even stole our wealth
Our resources
Re-represented our representation
Re-represented our reputation
And misrepresented all of the above
Tore apart our family
They r the prison within the ism
They fucked with our intelligence
Our reverence
Tried 2 steal our reciprocity
Tampered with our sanity
We've become a fictional people
We think that
They think that
We're all equal
What an illusion
We pray to myths
We've been exploited by everybody
Mind
Soul and body
Somebody
Everybody
Is fuckin' with my physical,
Psychological/and spiritual body
Somebody is fucking wit my mind
It's a honky on my shoulder
Should I kill it?
We need 2 do positive affirmations n the mirror
I love myself and I won't b anyone else
I love myself and I won't b anyone else
I love myself and I won't b anyone else
I love myself and I won't b anyone else
I love myself and I won't b anyone else
I won't be Asian
I won't be Mexican
I won't be European

Uncensored!

The role of law and constitution is institution
Our concepts has constructs
Constructs that abduct u
Define u
Redefine u
Confine u
Detain u
Class constructs
Racial constructs
Political constructs
Social constructs
Economic constructs
Cultural constructs
Constructs 2 categorize u
As lower class
Middle class
Upper class
THEY CAN ALL KISS MY ASS
The ancestors often come back 2 me
They tell me
Somebody is fucking wit my mind
And we've gotta get beyond this shit!

Uncensored!

Senses

Ears can't be bound 2 simple rhetoric
Eyes can't be bound 2 rhetoric of binded paper
Truth doesn't have 2 be heard
Flesh doesn't have 2 be touched 2 be stimulated
Spirituality is not taught
It's not an idiom
Ology
Perception
Belief system
Theory
Or paradigm
It just is
I am that stone or mineral that energy exist within
Familiar with the spirit within it
The matter that sustains it
We can be Moor
We are like cattle that settle for mediocrity
Tongue wishes all and desires
But only when action 2 b is not contradictory
Universal law is more than just universal
We are a tunnel way
Hoping 2 one day truly overstand what really exists
Grids
Dimensions
Spirits
Doorways 2 the soul
Kundalini
Chakras
Passages to immortality
Gates within our own bodies
Celestial bodies
How ignorant of man 2 think we are the only being
Can't c n the light or the darkness
Afrikans still scared 2 encounter their melanin

Uncensored!

Allowing recessive genes to abduct u
Even diabolical man can't colonize DNA code
Can't colonize genetic memory bank
Rewritten words can't rewrite what's already n me
So forget or pretend 2 forget
But the ancestors r calling u
Feel the power beyond material
Stop imitating the anti-spiritual mask
Alienating self from antique existence
The beginning 2 be manifested only 2 be dissected
Only ignorant zealot
Falsifies truth for ego's masturbation and prejudice
Minds capability thinks beyond us
A tangible existence
Not bound 2 blindness
Procreate ohms n the universe
The all n one energy
From micro 2 macro we exist
Outside the physical
Infinitely

Uncensored!

Battle Cry

This isn't a hate speech
This is a love speech
I'm not here to entertain you
I'm here to teach
This ain't a poem
This is a battle cry
We at war and I'm seeing
Too many of our people die
You been stepped on and lied to
Beaten until your souls turned black and blue
Taught to disrespect the women who
Gave birth to you
Then you were drugged up and numbed up
and taught to kill each other
So they didn't have to
Can't you see this is GENOCIDE
and non-violence under these conditions is SUICIDE
You gotta protect your people if you want to survive
Cause there's this world wide conspiracy
Called white supremacy
Designed to kill you and me
What price are you willing to pay to be free
How many of you know that revolution
Is not turning the other cheek
I know some of you are scared to bleed
You say you wanna change things peacefully
We been peaceful
You can't leave your fate to the enemy
Some of you have been fooled into joining the military
Sent off to kill your own people
So the KraKKKas could make money
That's why I say George Bush is Willie Lynch
And divide and conquer is still working
Watch him turn House Negroes against Field Negroes

Uncensored!

and send Field Negroes to kill Sand Negroes
Young against old
Man against woman
Rich against poor
Hate yourselves and each other but
Love your president
Go on and fight for your government
Your flag
Your country
Your way of life
Your freedom
You have lost your goddamn minds!
This isn't a hate speech
This is a love speech
I'm not here to entertain you
I'm here to teach
This ain't a poem
This is a battle cry
We should start taking there lives
Cause I'm sick of seeing our people die
and if they had rhythm
I'd make them dance to
Bullets at their feet
Laugh and ask them how they like defeat
Fuck' em
Give them hell until we're free
We need to all pick up gats
Make guns clap
It's time to take our streets back
And trust me it'll work if we do it collectively
That's why Willie never taught us unity
He knew you'd be fighting him
So he taught you to fight me
I wrote this piece for the few that feel me
The riders who will stomp and spit on their flag with me
Souljahs gear up we taking everything
and we'll make this police state fall just like Israel will
We'll fight the Zionists pigs until we're free

Uncensored!

Then let the Palestinian youth
Write Israel's eulogy
Don't hide from the devils
Who tommy-gun us in our sleep
Wake up the knives are still in our backs and the cuts are deep
But we're still standing so don't welcome defeat
It hurts to see my people weak
Do you know that we're royalty?
Our ancestors were kings and queens
The blood in our veins is rich and sweet
We own this
While we were building civilizations
They were living like savages in caves
Eating each others flesh decayed
We grew food
Built communities and absorbed the sun rays
Shit, we created the way that we count the days!
Now it's time for them to count their days
It's up to y'all how long y'all wanna be slaves
But me
I'm ready to take this back cause we own it
They just stole it
This isn't a hate speech
This is a love speech
I'm not here to entertain you
I'm here to teach
This ain't a poem
This is a battle cry
We at war and I'm sick of seeing
Our people die

Written by
Azadeh

AmeriKKKan History 101

Lied about the insurance policy on the slaves
Lied about creation
Lied about A.I.D.S
Lied about Tuskegee experiments
Black Wall Street
Cointelpro
Crack
Genocide
Terrorism
Plan crashes
Civilization
Indian Reservations
Depopulation
Population
Lied about art
Lied about the Black Madonna
White one too
Lied about the Nuwbas
Queen Nannie
Black August
Gorbachev
Kosovo
General Paten
Westmorland
Japanese Internment Camps
Ghetto Concentration Camps
Lied about melanin
Lied about 3rd eyes and black dots
Lied about
Pineal
Pituitary
And hypothalamus glands
Lied about
Halloween

Thanksgiving
Christmas
Easter
Valentine's Day
Veterans Day
Labor Day
Memorial Day
They lying everyday
Sold fairytales on Abner Louima
Told fairytales on David Koresh
Lied about the Cold War
Iran, Iraq, Syria, Turkey, Korea
Lied about Sept.11th
Central Intelligence
Elmina Castle
Goree Island
Jim Crow
Omecs
Mayas
Aztecs
Panama
Afrikanized bees
Stonehenge
Stem cell research
AZT
Still lying about Christopher Columbus
The Arawaks
Still won't tell the truth about the power elite
Lied about Mossaddeq
Arbenz of Guatemala
South Vietnamese President Diem
Salvador Allende
Manual Noriega
Still won't tell the truth about F.E.M.A
Statue of Liberty
Hegemony
Monarchy
Lie about being privileged

Uncensored!

Bush is lying about everything
Tell me what he's not lying about
Ashcroft
Cheney
Colin Powell
Condoleezza White Rice
Tony Blair too
Nixon Watergate was nothing new
Washington lied
Jefferson
Lincoln
Kennedy
Reagan
Both Roosevelts lied
Name me one president who ain't lied
Name one
I dare u
They lied about oral sex internships
N the White House
Al Qaeda
Technology
Gross National Product
The Zapatistas
Bay of Pigs
Bunker Hill
World War 1
World War 2
Enron
Elections
Coalition of the willing
Unwilling
Who got weapons of mass destruction?
Who don't?
Why they don't and why they won't?
Lied about the aspirin factory n Sudan
Remember Fred Hampton
Report on Kennedy assassination was imagination
Questioned Mark Furman under oath

He lied
Police Departments lie
Governments lie
Fairytales land us n jail
Ask Geronimo Pratt
When they gone free Mumia and H. Rap Brown
Still lying about the Palestinians
Islam
The Resurrection
The Deficit
Greece
Rome
Britain
Lied about Biko
Mandela
Apartheid
Lying about N.A.T.O
World Health Organization
International Trade Agreements
Bank Statements
Foreign Policy
But the policy is only foreign to u and me
And who decided Jesus would be white?
Lied about the so-called Untouchables
Aborigines
Nile Valley Civilization
The Aga people
Lied about SARS
Their secret files lie too
Lie about democracy
Integration
Diversity
Multiculturalism
Ethnic cleansing
Won't tell the truth about their occupancy in caves
Who tried to civilize them only to be made slaves?
Still lying about who the real Jews are
Who funded slavery?

Uncensored!

Lie about the Federal Reserves
New World Order
Tsunamis
Guantanamo Bay
Religion
Education
Racism
Homeland Security Bill
Patriots Acts
Legislation
Land Grab
Operation Northwood
Operation Chaos
Operation Hoodwink
Operation Falcon
Operation Nutcracker
The media is lying
CBS
NBC
ABC
FOX
And all of their affiliates are lying
These mothafuckas are lying!

"When you allow someone else to define your History
It will be a microcosm of
<u>*BULLSHIT*</u>*!"*

Sadiki Bakari

Epilogue

It is my intention that the reader of Butt Naked, Raw & Uncensored recognizes the state of emergency and urgency that we are in as a people and I also wanted to engage the Afrikan into his or herself and engage everyone else into the Afrikan. It's not often that the world actually see through the eyes of the victimized unless they're Jewish. I hope that reading this book has given you some clarity to our historical and present existence as well as spiritual, psychological and political insight into where future generations may be headed. Hopefully you have learned more about your internal self and will be able to deconstruct the religious and educational dictum created by white psychopaths. This book through essays, retrospective, articles, an interview and poems dealt with every aspect of Global <u>White</u> Supremacy as Neely Fuller so eloquently coined the term. I know it is most imperative that we truly overstand the many problems that exist. That is why I opened the book with the essay entitled *Guilty* to deal with Amerikkkas' historical and present *terrorist acts*. Now I hope that you will research and probe diligently into our solutions for freedom.

Education, economics, entertainment, labor, law, politics, religion, sex and war are all constructs within global white supremacy. When carried out structurally and institutionally these are all individually war crimes against humanity internationally. It is not enough to say our resistance is against fascism, imperialism and capitalism. The exploiters and owners of these systems must be identified. The system of Global <u>White</u> Supremacy didn't create itself. We must not be afraid to identify terrorism and say it is white people and their corporations and government directly or indirectly who are the past and present villains of this hegemony used to maintain their status quo. If you are not fighting against it then you are part of the problem. Their lackeys are simply gatekeepers and magicians to facilitate the illusion. The industrial prison complex is big business and the new cotton plantation, as well as corporate Amerikkka itself. How does it feel to be part of a pseudo democracy and civilization dictated by psychopaths?

The greatest rebellion will be in our spirit and psyche. We must change the way we think and act as a people. It's time to educate ourselves outside of the western educational system, stop worshiping white images, symbols and religions, realize that western culture is neurotic and psychopathic in the least and most importantly unite as a people on the basis of commonality like oppression. This system has never been beneficial to Afrikans. Now our own inner struggle is the manifestation of God/Goddess state or the well-trained, constructed, psychologically distorted, socially reared minstrel, self-hating, assimilation-minded, integration-minded Negro. Suppress that inner Negro and release your greatest weapons of mass destruction (your black sperm and your spirit)! The days of bowing our heads and getting on our knees and praying are over. The days of trying to compromise our way to freedom are over. Faith doesn't breed action, only laziness. The system, white folk and people who think like white folk are precise in their systematic oppression and dehumanization of humanity. They still see us as *NIGGERS* no matter how badly one tries to assimilate or integrate. The seizure of power or continued powerlessness is amongst us. The current system will not reform or change. According to Dr. Bobby E. Wright, "The psychopath is an individual who is constantly in conflict with other persons or groups. He is unable to experience guilt, is completely selfish and callous and has no respect for the rights of others." White Amerikkka and whites (historically) are the psychopaths I have documented throughout these writings extensively. You can't disprove this. The Amerikkkan dream is just that, a dream. Amerikkka the psychopath is a reality! The call to action is there must be a new system implemented for the people by the people. In the final analysis we will be led by truth or perish due to ignorance. Either way, only we can determine our fate. *MAA KHERU*!

Sadiki Bakari

About the Author

Sadiki Bakari was born in Cleveland, Ohio and relocated to Los Angeles, California at the age of four. He is the son of poverty parents who worked their way to the upper middle class. His religious background often contradicted his spirit and logic. As a promising potential professional athlete, Sadiki found a sense of freedom in athletics until recognizing the racism and politics involved in its corporate structure, "RUN NIGGER RUN." The streets, the university and corporate AmeriKKKa gave Sadiki an empirical and field research look at the state of Afrikans and the inhumane and corrupt sense of AmeriKKKan culture and socio-politics. His leadership qualities have always been in the forefront even as a youth. He is a child of the sun, descendant of the original people, a son, a father, a brother, mysterious to some, selfless, a servant of the people, a Hip-Hop kid, a throw back to the 70's, an angelic being, creator, writes red, black and green words that does drive-bys on red, white and blue words. He is a lover of nature, world traveler and a free spirit but don't cross him because his tongue is a sword and cuts deep into one's psyche and emotional state. He is loved as well as hated but most importantly well respected.

Sadiki says that his ancient fore parents twisted the original lock, uttered the first words of wisdom and tamed evil spirits. He often senses their spirit in his intuition and heightened states of energy. Their protection gives him strength and solace while fighting his own contradictions and the contradictions within the system. True humanity will always be a work in progress just as this person is. This activist, writer, lecturer, poet, and author promises to always give you the truth no matter what the repercussions are. It is his duty to live up to the manifestation of the *MAA KHERU* for our ancestors who shed blood and dared to fight and struggle against oppression endlessly for our freedom!

Uncensored!